The Rise of Regional

Christopher Harvie is Professor of British Studies at the University of Tübingen, Baden-Württemberg, Germany and has been Visiting Fellow at Merton and Nuffield Colleges, Oxford, at Edinburgh and at Strathclyde. He has written broadcasts and made appearances on British and German television, commentates on politics and history for BBC Radio Scotland and BBC World Service, regularly writes on European politics for *The Scotsman*, and contributes to *The Guardian* and *New Statesman*.

His previous books include: *Scotland and Nationalism*, 1977, 1994; *No Gods and Precious Few Heroes: Scotland 1914–1980*, 1981, 1987, 1993; *'The Centre of Things': Political Fiction in Britain from Disraeli to the Present*, 1991; and *Cultural Weapons: Scotland and Survival in a New Europe*, 1992. He was a contributor to Kenneth O. Morgan (ed.) *The Oxford Illustrated History of Britain*, 1984, and contributing editor (with Arthur Marwick, Charles Kightly and Keith Wrightson) to *The Dictionary of British History*, 1980.

Historical Connections

Series editors:
Tom Scott, University of Liverpool
Geoffrey Crossick, University of Essex
John Davis, University of Connecticut
Joanna Innes, Somerville College, University of Oxford

The Rise of Regional Europe

Christopher Harvie

London and New York

First Published 1994
by Routledge
11 New Fetter Lane, London EC4P 4EE

Simultaneously published in the USA and Canada
by Routledge
29 West 35th Street, New York, NY 10001

Typeset in Times by
Ponting–Green Publishing Services, Chesham, Bucks

Printed in England by Clays Ltd, St Ives plc

British Library Cataloguing in Publication Data
A catalogue record for this book is available from the
British Library.

Library of Congress Cataloging in Publication Data
Harvie, Christopher T.
    The rise of regional Europe/Christopher Harvie.
        p.   cm. – (Historical connections)
    Cover title: The Rise of Regional Europe.
    Includes bibliographical references and index.
    1. Europe–Politics and government–1989-
    2. Europe–Civilisation–20th century.
    3. Regionalism–Europe   I. Title.
    II. Title: Rise of regional Europe.   III. Series.
    D2009.H36   1993
    940.5–dc20   93–13819

ISBN 0–415–09523–9

Contents

Series editors' preface

Historical Connections is a new series of short books on important historical topics and debates, written primarily for those studying and teaching history. The books will offer original and challenging works of synthesis that will make new themes accessible, or old themes accessible in new ways, build bridges between different chronological periods and different historical debates, and encourage comparative discussion in history.

If the study of history is to remain exciting and creative, then the tendency to fragmentation must be resisted. The inflexibility of older assumptions about the relationship between economic, social, cultural and political history has been exposed by recent historical writing, but the impression has sometimes been left that history is little more than a chapter of accidents. This series will insist on the importance of processes of historical change, and it will explore the connections within history: connections between different layers and forms of historical experience, as well as connections that resist the fragmentary consequences of new forms of specialism in historical research.

Historical Connections will put the search for these connections back at the top of the agenda by exploring new ways of uniting the different strands of historical experience, and by affirming the importance of studying change and movement in history.

Tom Scott
Geoffrey Crossick
John Davis
Joanna Innes

Preface and acknowledgements

The first sight of the town of Veere, through the curtains of poplars which flank the straight highways of Zeeland, is of the filigree spire of the Stadthuis. Then, once round a corner, riding above the tree-level like an elephant through rushes, rears the bulk of the Groote Kerke. The Groote Kerke is a shell; it was burnt out in 1686; of the seaport of 5,000 people only a hundred or so houses survive. Two of these are the Schotse Huizen, for between 1541 and 1796 Veere was the 'staple' for Scots trade with Europe. In one of these a letter of 1686 instructs John Buchan, agent, to remind Dutch merchants of their obligation to trade through Veere and not to transfer their custom to the port of Rotterdam. The letter came not from the Scottish parliament, but from the Convention of Royal Burghs, another estate of the country's complex constitution, which still thrives. Outside the old fortress, now a hotel, the yachts flit across the Veere Lake, once an arm of the sea. The man who recommended me to come here was Buchan's twentieth-century successor, Grant Baird, Director of 'Scotland Europa', the Scottish Office's new Brussels representation, whose weekend retreat this is.

Another country, another Scotsman. Gordon Craig, in his subtle and sympathetic study, *The Germans*, attempting to find reasons for authoritarian distortions of the German intellect, finds some roots in the damage inflicted on the country in the Thirty Years War, 1618–1648. In this period, he writes, the population of the Duchy of Württemberg fell from 400,000 to 166,000 (Craig 1991: 25). The evidence for this stems, according to S. H. Steinberg, from a Württemberg inquest of 1652, in which the representative chamber clocked up a damage claim totalling 118,742,864 guilders:

> The Württemberg estates were the most powerful as well as the most vocal institution of their kind in the whole of Germany: they would

certainly not let pass an occasion for the most extravagant claims on
the purse of their Duke.

(Steinberg 1966: 104)

These two instances make the point that relations between political
units have not always been determined by national governments.
Regional institutions stand behind the nation, can often intervene in its
affairs with considerable effect, and may conceivably survive it. This
brief and unsatisfactory book is about them. It is brief because it has to
fit into a series, against a strict time-and-word limit. It is unsatisfactory
because the subject, once placed centre stage, threatens to invert the
hierarchies of conventional history without (so far) putting anything
coherent in their place.

To type 'EUROPEAN REGIONALISM' into the Libertas database at the
London School of Economics and press the return key, is to conjure up
no less than 150 references. Among them there is, so far, no 'regional
history': there is a vast range of regional disciplines – geographical,
ethnological, sociological, political, economic, anthropological – but
somehow these contrive to speak not to but *alongside* one another,
rather like guests at a badly organised dinner party. Nationalism as a
discourse is palpably present, yet on closer inspection its familiarity
seems to carry it through powerful inconsistencies, points where the
ethnic or the economic seem to subvert it. The regional and its
Doppelgänger the civic have been around far longer and caused less
trouble. Perhaps some of Europe's present difficulties stem from this
relative lack of dramatics. While nationalism bellows from the stage,
they are still getting their memory, and their act, together.

Whether they will do so in time, remained dubious while this book
was being written. The forward march to a federal Europe was slowed
by the Danish and French referenda on the Maastricht Treaty; Britain's
and Italy's economic difficulties made them leave a crumbling currency
union. Maastricht was then interpreted as offering a greater degree of
'subsidiarity', but to whom? To provinces and regions? What Germany,
the Leviathan of the Communities, thought was surely important. Of the
two economic invalids, a British government elected by 31 per cent of
the voters persisted with centralism, while in Italy the fast-growing
Northern League patently preferred European federalism and the
dismemberment of its own country to the perpetuation of Cavour's
crumbling, corruption-riddled creation.

That apart, was nationalism staging a comeback? Obviously there
was a difference between the European states – fortunate regions which

had made it to legislative autonomy – and the four fifty-million plus 'powers'. 'Nation-state' revivals in any of these looked remote. Post-referendum France seemed as inscrutable as the features of President Mitterand, yet the most powerful 'yes' votes came from those areas in which regional consciousness was most advanced: Brittany, Rhône-Alpes, Alsace-Lorraine. French nationalism, like German nationalism and British nationalism, had become, by contrast, a vehicle for the racist and populist extreme right. The British government, sensitive to the fact that its experiment in 'a free economy and a strong state' had been a social and economic failure, could not hide from the Edinburgh summit delegates a crumbling monarchy and a host country noisily wanting out of the United Kingdom. Whether the 'national' could again overtake the federal was, to say the least, debatable.

This book was commissioned by Claire L'Enfant of Routledge on the assurance that I could unravel the outlines of an interpretation of the recent European past which would show the importance of the regional theme. Her help has been generous beyond the bounds of editorial duty. Various invitations to lecture on associated themes – on poetry and regional culture at Tübingen University's Blaubeuren Colloquium in 1990; on German federalism to the Transpennine Conference in Hull in May 1991; on British regionalism to a *Political Quarterly* symposium at Coleg Harlech, and on what I christened 'bourgeois regionalism' to the Social History Conference at Glasgow and the Rauischholzhausen Colloquium in 1992 – led to the confidence that only a swift editing job would be required to produce a complete and convincing argument. This was, of course, far from being the case. The book took on its own shape and dictated a far more severe programme from its author. In this I was helped by two additional assignments: the *European History Quarterly* asked me to review the eight-volume series of *Comparative Studies on Governments and Non-Dominant Ethnic Groups in Europe, 1850–1940*, commissioned by the European Science Foundation; and in 1991 I contributed to a study of older industrial regions organised by the Centre for the Study of the European Working-Class Movement at the Ruhr-University Bochum. These provided near-definitive treatments of the two polarities of the regional issue, the ethnic and the economic, and my gratitude to their collective authorships knows no bounds.

What I have tried to do is the following, in a book that is essentially thematic in its first four chapters, and concerned with economic and political manoeuvre in post-war Europe in the last two. I have tried first to define the chances and the possible pitfalls of the present situation; then to estimate the degree to which these alter the way in which we have traditionally surveyed the European past, by stressing the continuing debate between the ethnic and the industrial. This leads to a reappraisal of the actors of national politics in the context of the regional theme, and then a consideration of the persistence of types of civic and internationalist discourse. The last two chapters deal with the transactions that have created 'bourgeois regionalism', the working-out of its politics in modern Germany, the only state so far to have integrated federal and European politics, and its implications for the future of Europe.

As a Scot living and working in Germany, and spending most of my vacations in Wales, I found that my own situation provided a position of some interpretative value. Baden-Württemberg has been the leading force of 'bourgeois regionalism'; Scotland has contributed probably more than any other place to the theory of civic government, from Fletcher of Saltoun and Adam Ferguson to Patrick Geddes; and Wales has thrown itself into its role as a European region with great energy. All have made their informal contribution to a project which depends on picking people's brains, as well as reading, and I am particularly grateful to the following for assistance, information, and argument: Lord Annan, Dr Neal Ascherson, Peter Aspden and Dr Huw Richards of the *Times Higher Education Supplement*, Prof. Grant Baird of Scotland Europa, Prof. Logie Barrow, John Milne and Douglas MacLeod of BBC Scotland, Robin Bennett of the Scottish Legal Action Group, Prof. Kevin Boyle, Dr Elmar Brandt of the Goethe-Institut, Alfred Braun of the Friedrich-Ebert-Stiftung, Iain Frater of the British Council, Profs Philip Cooke and Dai Smith of Cardiff University, Wayne David MEP, Elke Berger of the Deutsch-Englische Gesellschaft, George Kerevan and Mark Lazarowicz, Dr Bob MacCreadie, Dr Christof Ellger, Ken Munro, Dr Neil Evans, Dr Alun Gwynedd Jones, Prof. Bill Fishman, David Fletcher of Transpennine, Dr Tom Gallagher, Martin Kettle and David Gow of the *Guardian*, John Osmond, Tom Nairn, Dr Roland Sturm, Paul Salveson, Peter Jones and Bob Campbell of the *Scotsman*, Prof. Michael Keating, Dr Rainer Schulze of the Ruhr-Universität Bochum, Prof. Hans-Gustav Klaus, Ursula Kimpel, Dr Thomas Kleinknecht, Clemens Ludwig, Douglas Lowndes and Sue Bennett, Dr Allan MacCartney, Prof. Bernard Crick, Prof. Kenneth Morgan, Dr Lindsay Paterson, Prof. Philip Williams, George Rosie, Alex Salmond MP, Helmut Schröder, Susanne Dinkelacker, Dr Gerd Schulten of the Europa-Institut, Tübingen, Brian Groom of *Scotland on Sunday*, Dr Colin Smith of Scottish Enterprise, Prof. David Vincent, David Griffiths of the Welsh Development Agency, Prof. John Williams. In my office at Tübingen, Paddy Bort helped organise the two Freudenstadt Colloquia at which many of the above conversations occurred, and Carola Ehrlich typed much of the manuscript and organised the bibliography. My thanks to my wife Virginia and daughter Alison for their support and tolerance, and to my family in Scotland for their hospitality.

Working with Ned Thomas and John Barnie of *Planet: The Welsh Internationalist* (it has lived up to its subtitle) over the last five years has been a continual stimulus, and I dedicate *The Rise of Regional Europe* to them.

EUROPEAN REGIONS, 1993

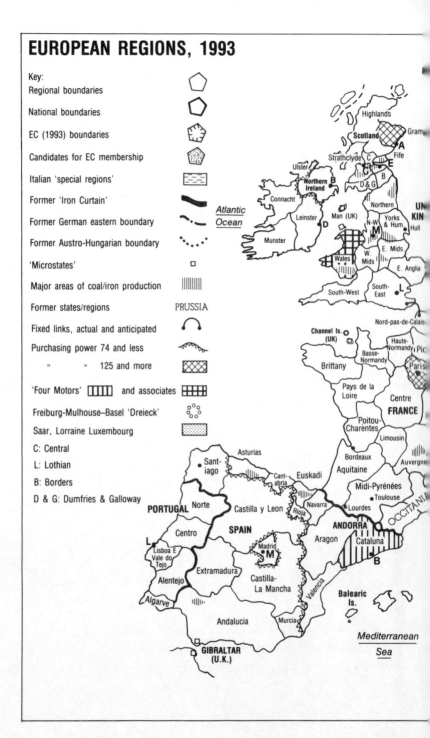

Key:

Regional boundaries	
National boundaries	
EC (1993) boundaries	
Candidates for EC membership	
Italian 'special regions'	
Former 'Iron Curtain'	
Former German eastern boundary	
Former Austro-Hungarian boundary	
'Microstates'	
Major areas of coal/iron production	
Former states/regions	PRUSSIA
Fixed links, actual and anticipated	
Purchasing power 74 and less	
" " 125 and more	
'Four Motors' [ITITI] and associates	
Freiburg-Mulhouse–Basel 'Dreieck'	
Saar, Lorraine Luxembourg	
C: Central	
L: Lothian	
B: Borders	
D & G: Dumfries & Galloway	

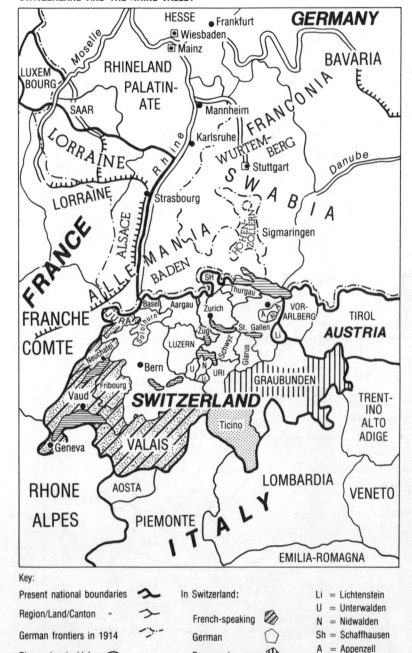

Key:

		In Switzerland:		
Present national boundaries			Li	= Lichtenstein
Region/Land/Canton "			U	= Unterwalden
German frontiers in 1914		French-speaking	N	= Nidwalden
		German	Sh	= Schaffhausen
Rivers (navigable)		Romansch	A	= Appenzell
Canals		Italian	Al	= Appenzell ausser Rhoden

1 Introduction
Europe and Its Regions Today

REGIONALISATION INTO REGIONALISM

In the late 1980s the idea of a 'Europe of the Regions' suddenly became politics. The European ideal revived with the passing of the Single European Act, and the process of governmental and policy integration accelerated. Confronted with federalism, the politicians of the German *Länder*, of the Spanish 'autonomous communities', and even, increasingly, of the French regional councils, discovered the 'principle of subsidiarity', and interpreted it as the devolution of powers from Brussels and Strasbourg not to a national but to a sub-national or regional level.

Most Westminster politicians looked at federalism and sulked patriotically, Britain being now the only substantial state within the European Communities which had no regional legislatures. But even here there were three anomalies. The Conservative government, having dismantled the English regional economic councils and withdrawn many powers from local authorities – an unparalleled process bound to provoke clashes with European institutions – was also anxious to settle the endemic conflict in Northern Ireland by *devolving* power. Second, there existed in the United Kingdom Jersey, Guernsey and the Isle of Man: three of Europe's eight micro-states, economically significant through their taxation laws. Finally, nowhere else in Western Europe was the regional issue so much one of 'national' consciousness, with the existence of 'stateless nations' – Scotland, Wales, Northern Ireland – whose devolved bureaucracies were only one aspect of highly developed and distinctive cultures and civil societies. Their discontent fulminated beneath the rhetoric of 'Britain' articulated by a government drawing its vote overwhelmingly from England 'south of the M25', influencing the regional government projects of the Labour party and the constitutional demands of Charter '88.

The European project contained a 'regional' element from its earliest stages but, significantly, the 'regional policy' defined by the first generation of EC legislation (1957–73), dealt with 'areas of the member countries which, for reasons of economic change, have obsolete, obsolescent or declining industries, and suffer from lack of investment and high unemployment' (Paxton 1984: 220). It was the pendant of a Common Agricultural Policy which aimed at stabilising and rendering politically harmless an inefficient peasant agriculture during the transition to a modern industrial regime; so the first 'recognised' regions were the Italian *Mezzogiorno* and south-western France (Clout 1987: 19). According to Alan Milward, the net result was the strengthening of the nation-state. 'Europeans' such as Jean Monnet, Paul-Henri Spaak and Luigi Einaudi might talk of the transfer of powers to Brussels accelerating the state's decline, but this remained rhetoric while states found that common action over agriculture or coal subsidies bought off the miners on the left and the peasants on the right, stabilising and strengthening their own identity (Milward 1992: 21–45).

With the accession of the United Kingdom and Ireland in 1973, a formal Community Regional Policy was adopted. The original 'regions' were joined by much of north and west Britain, north-western France and the whole of Ireland. In the same decade, violent upheavals in Ulster, Corsica and Euskadi (the Basque Country), and gentler political agitations elsewhere, gave the regional issue political salience. Sociological explanations, such as Michael Hechter's 'internal colonialism' thesis and Stein Rokkan's attempt at a typology of European regional evolution, slipped into the pabulum of academic conferences. Matters hung fire somewhat with the mid-1970s depression, the slowing-down of European integration, and the falling-off of support for nationalism in Scotland and Wales, but in the course of the 1980s, 'regionalism' not only revived but underwent an almost revolutionary change in definition (Hechter 1975; Rokkan 1980).

The regions seen as the reflex of a revived Euro-federalism were different. Like the rich. Far from being geographical anthologies of cultural particularism and social obsolescence, certain regions (largely but not exclusively drawn from the 'core', the London–Frankfurt–Milan–Paris quadrilateral, and including all three EC 'capitals': Strasbourg, Luxembourg and Brussels) now seemed the 'sharp end' of European consciousness: areas of sophisticated technology, environmental awareness, local democracy, and a culture and civil society which integrated the intimate and the cosmopolitan. This was articulated forcibly in 1989 by a politician typical of the new generation, the

Social Democrat Minister-President of the German Saarland, Oskar Lafontaine:

> *Rapprochement* and communication, the magic formulae of global-isation, don't mean, however, that we should surrender before the economic tendencies towards unification, standardisation and levelling-out. Our political will should aim at variety. We don't want, parallel to the development of world-wide compatible computer systems, an anonymous 'Mao-look'; we want the coexistence of local, regional, inter-regional and national sub-cultures, something which, in the case of the United States, has helped create wealth through the power and dynamism of cultural interaction.
>
> (Lafontaine 1989)

The new regions – I have elsewhere christened them 'bourgeois regions' (Harvie 1992) – were vividly and attractively present: in museums and architectural competitions, as fashion and publishing centres, in improved public transport, traditional tastes in food and drink. The last few years have not been good for London, Madrid and Rome, but they have benefited Glasgow as European Culture Capital in 1990, Barcelona with the 1992 Olympics, and Milan as a fashion centre. The regions were also seen – ambitiously – as prototypes for the nations struggling out of the debris of the Warsaw Pact: a type of political community which had to collaborate as much as it integrated.

The quickening pace of this 'Europeanisation' could not be detached from two things: the retreat from 'smokestack' industry, and the apparent victory of 'market economics' over traditional étatisme. But how different the 'social marketism' of Europe was from dogmatic classical economics was seen in the last battle of Margaret Thatcher in 1990 when, determined to defend the 'integrity' of Britain against Brussels as well as against 'enemies within', she was struck down by her own party. European federalists saw the market as something that would in due course recede, exposing a 'civic' level of communal decision-making. Mrs Thatcher somehow assumed that a minimal society could co-exist with a coercive, centralised state (Crouch and Marquand 1989). The Maastricht Summit's desire to hold by the 'principle of subsidiarity' was claimed as a success by the British government, but most of Europe regarded it as intensifying the devolution of decision-making to a regional level, and favoured the creation of a 'regional tier' within the central European institutions (*Maastricht Treaty* 1992). This could only menace further the future of the conventional defence-based nation-state.

Political scientists have already put together a formidable secondary literature on the movement and its recent evolution. Perhaps this reflects the regionalism of their own 'spiritual home', the United States and Canada; the evolution of the 'automobile city' to the dimensions of a smallish European state (Los Angeles covers about half the area of Wales); the drift of power from the Atlantic seaboard to California; the impact of the oil wealth of Texas or Alberta; the movement towards autonomy in Quebec, and the occupation of American space by new, and 'unmelting' ethnic groups. Yet the history of the civic, regional and culture-nation entities in Europe and their ethos – which will obviously influence the history of Europe as it will come to be written if the movement is successful – remains obscure (Keating 1988).

The chief boosters of the 'Europe of the regions' didn't figure in the books of the 1970s: neither Lombardy nor Rhône-Alpes, nor Baden-Württemberg. Yet it is difficult to separate the cultural, economic, and propagandist elements of the new regionalism, and to subject it to the same sort of critique which is now being levelled against the 'conventional' nation-state. No wonder the political scientist David Coombes could write in 1990, that

> 'Regionalism' as political doctrine verges on the absurd, failing to distinguish between the contrary values of national separatism or irridentism, on the one hand, and the general de-centralisation of state authority, on the other.
>
> (Coombes 1991: 148)

Common to all the new regions is the *fact* of political presence. They are not claimants for provincial self-government; they exercise it, or *appear* to exercise it, despite wildly-differing resources. To take two areas of 5 million population, the 'staff' of the elected Regional Council of Rhône-Alpes is 200; that of the unelected Scottish Secretary 14,000 (Colletis 1993; Linklater and Denniston 1992: 354). They are not 'problem' regions of peasants, industrial workers, and the unemployed, but centres which are now rivalling their traditional 'metropolises' (Keating 1991; Schlenker 1987; Gallagher 1991). Regionalisation, the chopping-up of problems into manageable areas, has now given way to a subjective and aggressive regionalism.

Baden-Württemberg (as addicted to diminutives as Scotland) coyly calls itself the *Ländle* or 'wee country', or *Musterländle* or 'wee showplace country', but now refers to Stuttgart as the *Neckarmetropole*. In the late 1980s, its government contributed to the voodoo of inter-regional high technology with its 'Four Motors' alliance with Rhône-Alpes, Cataluña, and Lombardy, and its former Minister-President Lothar Späth outlined this sort of set-up as a clear alternative to the existing Europe of sovereign states. We are therefore dealing not so much with a revolt against the central state, as an attempt to dismember it and rearticulate its components in quite new ways (Nairn 1991).

A NEW PARTICULARISM?

Attacks on the regionalist *fait accompli* were being made before political uncertainty overtook the whole European project in the autumn of 1992. Martin Kettle, the Editor of *Guardian Europe*, saw 'bourgeois regionalism' as a regression from existing nationalism, as clever special pleading on behalf of regions that had already concentrated in themselves a disproportionately large amount of the investment and the organisational structures of European capitalism. Their 'distinctive consciousness' lay more in their affluence than in any cultural identity. Their autonomy was like that of wealthy Americans who isolate themselves from the social problems of their cities behind barbed wire, whose political expression was traditionally the conservative rallying cry of 'states' rights'.

Dysfunctions in regional political systems – corruption scandals in many German *Länder* and in Milan, the unending Mafia saga of Sicily – also suggest that their elites may be less autonomous, or democratic, than subordinate to and manipulated by forms of multinational, cartel-ised capitalism, in a sort of 'particularism of the affluent'. Regionalism may be a means of politicians concealing their operations from the attentions of national or European newspaper or broadcasting media. Is the result, Baden-Württemberg or Rhône-Alpes Man, very different from Essex Man or Burbank Man – or from what Prague Man (once shot of the Slovaks) wants to be? Someone under rather than over the 'national' civic level, collusive with a government that protects its own narrow interests? And are the various pathological developments of nationalism – in ex-Jugoslavia or Northern Ireland – not a reaction to a 'cocooning' which is isolating the more affluent parts of Europe from the elements of solidarity inherent in the nation-state?

It is difficult to separate the cultural, economic and propagandist elements of 'regionalism', and to subject it to the same sort of critique which has come the way of the nation-state. This is partly because the ambiguity of the term means that it straddles several schools of interpretation, without integrating them. As part of state administration, region falls into 'old-fashioned' national history; as 'city-region', it is part of urban history; as 'culture-nation', it is part of the intensely political history of peoples aspiring to their own state; as 'industrial region', it is a central aspect of economic history. As we have already seen, the definitions don't stop there. Each has its own history and (it seems) a resistance to learning about anyone else's. But if we accept the telos as significant, it is surely necessary to make the attempt, and, with it, the connections. As E.M. Forster wrote of one of the greatest novels about a European region, Giuseppi de Lampedusa's *The Leopard* (1957), about the fate of the landed order in the Sicily of the *Risorgimento*, 'it shows how many ways there are of being alive'.

PINNING DOWN THE CONCEPT

The etymological history of 'region' suggests that any attempt from a British standpoint to establish the groundwork for a historical enquiry has to approach the subject in two main aspects. The first concerns itself with what the concept actually means. If the region is to be classed, as the Swiss political philosopher Denis de Rougemont defined it, as 'the space for civic participation in which man comes alive to the world and to himself at the same time', then we are entering the realm of metaphysics (de Rougemont 1977, 1983: 219). For the sociologist Anthony Giddens, the concept has also this fundamental quality, being a *foyer* for social action extending from the family dwelling to the nation-state (Giddens 1984: 120–43). Taken in the more strictly political sense of the field of action of hegemonic groups, the region or the city-region has a far longer track-record than the nation. Europe was dominated, as Fernand Braudel points out in *Civilisation and Capitalism*, for over five centuries by city-states – the Hanse, Venice, Amsterdam – against a century and a half by nation-states (Braudel 1979, 1985).

But what we are strictly concerned with – for boundaries have to be set somewhere – is the evolution of the regional concept from the period of national unification in the mid-nineteenth century to the present. How much has this been geographical, cultural, economic, political? How has it been affected by the major upheavals of the twentieth century? What have been the main literary and theoretical *démarches*?

This raises the factual corollary: how have the sub-nation-state units of European government been called into being? What powers have been vested in them? How have their politics functioned? Have they, in fact, constituted an alternative to the relationships of sovereign states? Are they creating intra-European relationships which, perhaps, provide stronger ties – in ecological or functional terms – than those which have bound the regions to the 'mother-country'? Or are they a wealthy Euro-suburbia insulating itself from unwelcome problems?

Further to this are two national problematics, which will be returned to at intervals – not simply because the author lives in both! Germany was traditionally, in contrast to France, the more decentralised as a great power, with twenty-six kingdoms, princely states and urban republics functioning as part of the Empire until 1918, and thereafter (rationalised into nineteen states in a republican form) as part of the Weimar settlement. The Nazis abolished the *Länder*, and replaced all elected politicians with *Gauleiter*, party functionaries. After 1945, new *Länder* were imposed by the Allies as the successor framework to the Third Reich, and since the enactment of the Basic Law in 1949, the Federal Republic has been the great pioneer of federalism within Europe. More recently, however, it has also been seen as the ailing Leviathan of the European Communities, overgoverned and over-burdened with debt, attempting to mediate between the almost patho-logical prosperity of Baden-Württemberg and Hesse on one hand, and the depression of the *Neuen Bundesländer*. These now include, in Thuringia, the poorest region in the EC: its GDP per capita only 30 per cent of the European average, against Portugal's 50 per cent (Stares 1992: 55–93; Schöneweg 1993: 2). Does the recrudescence of right-wing populism show that German bourgeois regionalism thus has been no match for either traditional nationalism or traditional particularism, even when modified by federal union?

In Britain, we appear to have a paradox: a polity without any vestige of federal authority; a highly centralised state. Yet a strong sense of separate identity within the four nations has taken two areas, Scotland and Northern Ireland, to a point at which secession seems more plausible than a continuation of the status quo. At the same time, the British record of uninterrupted constitutional government, the flexibility of its conventions, and the dialogue between the political traditions of its nations, acted as a consistent reservoir of evidence for decentralist initiatives, and a refuge for decentralist thinkers, from Jean-Jacques Rousseau to E.F. Schumacher. For the future: is some form of federalism possible and practicable – crucially, within the English regions – which can stabilise the UK situation, and integrate it within European institu-tions? If it is not granted, will the dialogue of province and metropolis, which past cultural critics repeatedly praised, reach a condition of stasis?

2 Rewriting the history

SUBVERTING EDUCATIONAL NATIONALISM

Regional history subverts traditional 'school history', oriented round the nation-state and its institutions. In a century dominated by world wars and their social, economic and cultural implications, we have taken the latter for granted. But the Second World War ended nearly fifty years ago, and the Treaty of Rome was signed in 1957, in a Europe closer to that of Edward VII and Wilhelm II than to the present situation: pre-nuclear, pre-automobile, pre-contraception, pre-television, pre-computer. The present comes at us unannounced. In a 'state of the art' collection of essays on pre-1945 Europe, the shadow of war is everywhere. Urbanisation and welfare are marginalised; of 'peacetime' prototypes, Sweden figures only in relation to its strategic importance, Switzerland not at all (Hayes 1992).

Reorientation seems difficult in Britain, particularly for English*men*. Bookstall and library shelves make clear the literary and emotional investment in the war years, something which implicitly defines foreigners as nationals ('the Germans', 'the French') but also 'freezes' British qualities – the Dunkirk spirit, living through the Blitz, and so on – less as living things than as a memory for an uncertain people. Sporting loyalties are more divided, only Olympic athletics having a 'British' identity, but this is the ironic result of being literally first in the field. Women, by contrast, seem to have a more flexible consciousness of place derived at one level from romantic and family-saga fiction, a regional speciality from the Brontës to Catherine Cookson; at another level, from the cosmopolitanism of fashion and cooking; at a third, from a professional tradition of learning and teaching foreign languages. Perhaps it's no accident that leading roles have been taken by women in environmentalism, the most regional of all political movements.

To tackle regionalism is to resume the themes of the Europe of 1910:

the civil politics of the last volume of the *Cambridge Modern History*. Comprehending the First World War elbowed out the political and industrial history of Belgium or Sweden; tracing the diplomatic and military pathways to it back to earlier centuries further marginalised such themes. Even when handled brilliantly by such as Fernand Braudel, the regional was 'early modern'. But technology, economic collaboration, multinational firms and global communications took over; historians were back with 'non-national' 'civics' and '*mentalités*': the reasons for their eclipse and, in the hands of such as Croce, Braudel and Pollard, for their recovery.

In this the British experience is anything but insular. 'The first industrial nation' was the paradigm of capitalist society on which Marxism, the great antithesis of liberal nationalism, was based. Further, by escaping invasion, the British 'flexible' constitution provided an example of continuity for more exciting and unstable countries. Quasi-federalism in continental Europe is often rooted in the experience of this 'unfederal' state. Finally, as part of the English linguistic community, Britain has been the 'interpreter's house' between Europe and the 'civics' and 'federalism' practised in the United States and in the Dominions.

INSTRUMENT INTO MOVEMENT

Anthony Giddens suggests how universal the 'region' concept is, but specific formations compel precise definitions. Just as federalism is understood by the Americans as centralisation, and by the Europeans as the opposite, their use of the word 'region' also diverges. A US region is something larger than the individual state: the 'regional movement' in literature after the First World War took in the northern part of the old Confederacy. In US external affairs, 'regional problem' means an area such as the Middle East which generates supra-national tension, or where continental polities collide. Given the scale of things in the USA – where most 'regions' are bigger than Scandinavia – one can see why.

But the European 'region' is awkward: at once vague, specific and spatially intimate. 'Land', 'pays', 'province', 'area', 'basin', 'arc' seem near-synonyms (Cochrane 1993). In the hands of Braudel in *The Mediterranean* (1949), 'region' might even be a synonym for the 'world' of a particular *mentalité*. In the *Oxford English Dictionary*, its original appearance is modest; its subsequent revisions formidable. In the Middle Ages, 'region' roughly corresponded to diocese, and *qua* legislative function, regional authorities have continued to concern themselves with socialisation: education, religion, culture and social control. But they have also been structured by topographical and industrial, as well as cultural and linguistic bounds. Unsurprisingly, this imprecise identity has – as much as nationalism – been projected by imagination and poetry as much as by rationalism and legalism. In Britain, where 'participative' regionalism is minimal, poets and novelists have been more than usually active as its 'unacknowledged legislators' (Harvie 1992: 75–9).

'Region' implies a *division* of government. First used to describe the internal arrangements of the Roman Empire, it fitted the neo-Aristotelian, medieval concept of a sovereignty divided between Christendom or the Empire and the local *polis*, but was more generous than the city-state, or imperial free city, whose privileges usually set it apart from the surrounding countryside (*OED* 1982: 1159f.; Kleinknecht 1985). Its modern meaning, however, derives from the subordinate administrative arrangements of the nation-state in the eighteenth and nineteenth centuries: for taxation, education and, above all, military purposes. In this, the region was suppressed by 'enlightened despots' in its localist/vernacular form, usually along with local aristocracies, churchmen and self-governing towns, their representative diets and estates. This process was continued by French revolutionaries, assaulting local jurisdictions and the Breton and Occitanian cultures, administering new *départements* by centrally appointed *préfets* (Mayo 1974: 13–58). The transformation of the Bonaparte family from supporters of the Corsican autonomist Pasquale Paoli into the symbols of French military imperialism was emblematic. Elsewhere – as in Prussia under vom Stein in 1808 – reformist regimes reacted to French conquest by restoring locality, on the 'British' pattern, as an 'efficient' but still restricted division of government (Schulze 1985: 201–10).

A regional 'movement' – as opposed to 'regionalisation' – requires public participation. This came late to the larger countries, although the First World War forced them to create bigger units than county, *département* or *Kreis* to organise agricultural production or civilian mobilisation (Stumann 1990: 217). This was repeated (at least theoretically) during the 'depression years', and again practically in the Second World War, although this was of dubious value, as it associated 'region' with bureaucratic control, requisitioning and rationing. The support of the Pétain government for regionalism, part of the furniture of a section of the French right since Count Gobineau, as well as a conscious surrender of national pride, helped to discredit the concept for a couple of decades after the war. The hand of restored Jacobinism was heavy against groups such as the Bretons. But by 1956, regions had become one of the subordinate levels of the Commissariat du Plan. The occasion of General de Gaulle's fall from power in 1969 was a proposal to give these a representative element, and a more elaborate version of this project was ultimately carried by President Mitterrand in 1982 (Dickinson 1967: 225–30; Ardagh 1986: 187–205). Over the same period the restoration of the German *Länder*, explicitly conceived as a means of weakening German nationalism – and so initially distrusted by the German people – proved an overwhelming success (Marsh 1992: 79).

THE INDUSTRIAL IMPERATIVE

This was, however, only one-half of the definition. The other aspect was the reorganisation of European societies which had rapidly become urban and industrial. Twenty per cent of the British population had lived in towns in 1800; over 70 per cent in 1900. Less than half of the land area of England lay outside their spheres of influence. Tackling their problems – water and sewage, labour supply, retail organisation, transport, housing – meant that city and region had to be considered together. This was the message of Patrick Geddes, for whom the congested, unhealthy 'conurbation' was the *palaeotechnic* city, and the planned 'city-region' the *neotechnic* city (Geddes 1915, 1949: Chapters 3 and 4). This interpretation underlay much of the theorising and later the executive action on regionalisation after the First World War.

By this time, liberal nationalism was under pressure from the revolutionary left, whose definition of 'socialist man' was literally utopian in depreciating local identity. But how accurate was any 'revolutionary' definition of industrialisation? The idea itself was an *ex-post-facto* rationalisation by the economist Auguste Blanqui in 1828, emphasised by Marx and Engels in their *Communist Manifesto* twenty years later. By 1990 it looked much less compelling. Not only had much of the Marxian world order fallen apart, but industrialisation and urbanisation had decoupled. City life in America had peaked and gone into decline. Types of self-sustaining suburban/rural industry and society had come into existence which did not require an urban 'core'. Elsewhere, mega-cities – São Paulo, Lagos, Bangkok – grew up on a minimal industrial base. Further, economic historians increasingly queried notions of 'industrial revolution' and instead postulated a much longer process of 'proto-industrialisation'. In this, agricultural regions gradually created an industrial base dominated by hand-work, while retaining rural settlement patterns and values. In this the survival of the mercantile city-state as a centre of capital, organisation and markets, remained important (Berg 1985: 315–19; Mendels 1972).

In North Italy and the Low Countries, and the Mark of Sweden, 'proto-industrialisation' was textile-based; in the Black Forest in Baden, the base was clock-making (Palm 1993). This combination of agriculture, crafts and manufacture even projected itself into the 'post-urban' industrialisation of rural Germany in the *Wirtschaftswunder*, in *Länder* such as Baden-Württemberg, with its 'part-time peasants' who also worked in high-technology factories, and into Italian 'microcapitalism'. Since proto-industrialisation depended on dispersed 'putting-out' communities rather than population concentrated in towns, it was regional rather than urban, and socially archaic rather than 'modernised', with the church, local customs, etc. still playing an important role. Even where urbanisation did in fact occur, rural loyalties could be carried over into urban life, as in Sweden or in Scotland, or combined with a tendency to emigrate, which in due course could introduce 'American' values of co-operation rather than class-confrontation.

Even if 'classical' industrialisation is now regarded more critically, it still was central for more than a century. The development of large-scale industry based on new sources of energy radically altered the political geography of nations, as coalfields and iron fields had no relationship to existing national boundaries. In Saxony and Bohemia, the coalfield crossed the frontier, likewise in Flanders and in Silesia. For some small states, industrial promotion compensated for political marginalisation: Saxony, for example, which lost two-thirds of its land area during the Napoleonic wars, threw itself into first textile-based and then capital-goods-based industrialisation, showing more initiative in this area than Prussia itself. In the Kingdom of Württemberg, wholly without iron ore or coal, the ministry set up a trade advisory department under Ferdinand Steinbeis in 1846 and a year later helped found the Royal Locomotive Works at Esslingen, specifically to build engines for the severe gradients of the line from Stuttgart to Munich. Esslingen cornered the market in heavy locomotives for nearly twenty-five years, and Württemberg went on to lead in the development of the motor industry. These developments were the result of what François Crouzet, contrasting eighteenth-century France with Britain, has called the 'challenges' of scarcity (Bramke 1993; Boelcke 1987; Crouzet 1966: 171).

The problem, however, was that industry required the participation of more powerful neighbours, both as markets and as sources of capital. This could happen within the nation-state, or through external influence. The Westphalian province of Prussia provides two contrasting examples. The rise of the iron and steel industries of the Ruhr was brought about by the military and railway demands of Prussia, which acquiesced in their cartelisation in order to retain the necessary spare capacity. So the social structure of the Ruhr's industrial elite was strongly concentrated, deeply bound up with national politics; its authority unquestioned in social and municipal affairs. In the Berg region to the south, around Barmen-Elberfeld, textile manufacture predominated, and there was a highly developed civic ethic, based both on protestant pietist individualism and on deliberate correspondences with the society of English textile towns like Manchester, to which the region was also linked by trade. The most famous by-product of this was Friedrich Engels' *Situation of the English Working Class* (1844) and its influence on Karl Marx, who (not surprisingly) stressed the internationality of capitalism (Petzina 1993: Reulecke 1993).

Specialised industrial areas often claimed a greater affinity with cognate regions in other countries than with the rest of their own nation. Glasgow was in this way closer in 1900 to other 'Atlantic' trading and industrial communities such as Liverpool, Barcelona or Philadelphia than to Edinburgh (Aspinwall 1980). As technologies grew more elaborate, or ran into trouble with obsolescence or market decline, capital had to be attracted from abroad. Manufacturing Belgium was in this way less autonomous than Holland – strongly agricultural outside the trading cities (Tamse 1985: 418–20). Moreover, the demand for labour was such that natural increase would fairly soon be overtaken by in-migration, which brought new ethnic and religious tensions (Bramke 1993). Another limiting factor was that, to guarantee an adequate infrastructure and social stability, industrial leaders would progressively have to dissipate their energies on non-industrial activities, such as politics, religious bodies and local government (Payne 1974).

LOCAL GOVERNMENT AND REVOLUTION

The influence of 'British' precedents – effective centralisation plus a convention of 'local self-government' – was confirmed by the shock of 1848. The revolutions contradicted Marx by being most violent in non-industrial countries – the Kingdom of the Two Sicilies, Hungary. In these, local government had been primitive, its reform postponed in favour of savage suppression of equally savage disturbances. But this risk could not be taken when new industrial areas were opened up, usually around the coalfields. A concentrated working population required control by military and police authorities, and some sort of precaution against public health disasters and mass unemployment (Langer 1969: 422).

Here Britain was the great prototype for continental liberals. Between

1830 and 1870, English borough councils changed from privileged corporations to 'interventionist' bodies. There was no philosophy behind this. The ruling Benthamite principles of reform (simultaneously systematic and philistine) implied units larger than the traditional parish – notably the Poor Law Unions (1834) – but these were restricted to local executive action, and kept to the rigid guidelines of a central office enforced by a travelling inspectorate. Smaller, parochial units were used for public health (1848) and education (1870) (Dicey 1905 : Lecture VI; Briggs 1958). The Benthamite programme provoked a backlash, articulated by figures like Toulmin Smith, David Urquhart and the Anti-Centralisation Union, 1854–7, although it was really as a result of the administrative incompetence of more traditional bodies in the Crimean War that the Benthamite General Board of Health was closed down in 1854 (Aspinwall 1982; Anderson 1967: 129–62).

Subsequently, British local government powers were gradually concentrated in the elective county councils, set up by the Conservative government in 1888. The *Radical Programme* of 1885 argued for a wholesale semi-federalisation of the country (*Radical Programme* 1885, 1971: 235–8, 248; Robson 1971: 233ff.), but Britain, escaping the shocks to which the continental powers were subjected, continued to subordinate local to central legislation, albeit without the 'prefectorial' arrogance of the French. This lesson was not lost on nations to whom unity was a recent experience. When the persistence of 'regionalism' was recognised, in the 1880s, it was treated with suspicion. The *Oxford English Dictionary* records 'that unfortunate "regionalism" of Italy' as an early usage (1881) in the *Manchester Guardian*, typical enough in being directed at one of Europe's less successful nation-states. Spanish regionalism made a similarly inauspicious early appearance: indeed, the first book on the subject, Alfredo Branas's *El Regionalismo* (1889) was written by a profoundly conservative Galician clericalist (Garrido 1991: 311).

In the early 1900s regionalism became more positive, with the growth of pluralist political theory of a New Liberal, Guild Socialist, Young Fabian or neo-Catholic sort – represented respectively by Harold Laski, G.D.H. Cole, H.G. Wells and G.K. Chesterton. Pluralism seemed to contradict nationalism of a self-referential sort, but came quite close to Mazzini's moralistic 'division of labour' between national units in undertaking a general work of enlightenment, at a time when nationalism had become increasingly identified with militarism and international tension (Nicholls 1973). In part, this was a 'qualified sovereignty' response to the challenge posed by Irish home rule to the centralised British constitution (Barker 1915: 177ff.). Indeed the geographer-polymath Geddes was the protégé of the Liberals' Scottish Secretary and Irish Viceroy, Lords Pentland and Aberdeen, and his *Cities in Evolution* (1913) had a direct influence on C.B. Fawcett's pioneering *The Provinces of England* (1921) (Meller 1990). The irony was that when the Irish crisis 'solved' itself through most of Ireland seceding in 1921, the issue disappeared from current politics (Fair 1980).

PARTICULARISM AND NATIONALISM

Britain was, in fact, typical of other European nations, its apparently explicit national ethos being shadowed by a dissenting discourse. British emotional loyalties, as projected abroad, were directed towards 'the sovereignty of the monarch in parliament'. The Scots tradition of a localised 'civic humanism', exemplified in particular by Andrew Fletcher of Saltoun's *Discourse on the Affairs of Scotland* (1697), which greatly appealed to Rousseau, was rejected by Adam Smith and David Hume, who regarded the large nation-state as the appropriate economic/political arena (Pocock 1975; Davie 1971: 27f.). Although Burke defended the rights within this *polis* of the Irish and the North American colonists, his hostility to any sort of fundamental alteration was such that an indivisible British 'nation', secured through defence and the party system, dominated the perception of Britain by most continental observers (Colley 1992). Mazzini considered that Ireland had no locus as a separate nation, and although Marx was more sympathetic to the Irish case, he and most of his disciples still considered the Irish an underprivileged minority in a unitary state (Nairn 1988: 127ff.).

This nationalism drew on the earlier ethos of Elizabethan and Jacobean England, made 'British' and 'protestant imperialist' by the Union of the Crowns in 1603 and the removal of the Scots court to London, and by the great cultural achievements of the period, Shakespeare's plays and the King James Bible. Marginalising the Scots ideal of 'semi-independence', this became, after Waterloo, as influential as French administrative rationalism in the Liberal hour in Europe (Williamson 1979: 5ff.; Phillipson 1968). Common to both was the assumption that the ultimate loyalties the state could call on were those for which men would be prepared to die, rather than pacific, small-scale localism – the patriotism of Grenville, Sidney, Nelson, rather than the trading ethic of the Fuggers, Finlays or Rothschilds: something ironically strengthened by the national development of utilities such as the railways.

This patriotic, militarist ethos was supplemented by a potent combination of culture, 'good manners' and romantic historical consciousness with a well-developed civil society and a robust if minimal government machine: something better adapted to the palates of continental conservatives than Jacobin rationalism. A blend of empiricism and social theory was imported by Scots philosophers and creative artists, notably James and John Stuart Mill, Sir Walter Scott and Thomas Carlyle, and this made the mixture even more potent (Harvie 1977: 130ff.). Scott, in particular, fused regionalism and large-scale nationalism to create the prototype of the 'national' imagination throughout Europe. Following Adam Ferguson, he reflected both the change in society from status to contract, and also a mounting apprehension of a social intercourse based on the 'cash-nexus'. His ideal of social settlement was realised in an 'ideal' region: the transformation of the Scottish border from a 'debatable land', scarred by endemic lawlessness, into a notable example of 'improvement' and 'cultivation' of a demotic but still securely deferential sort (Harvie 1983: 17–42).

He was also a neighbour of a cluster of the 'British' clerisy – Wordsworth, Coleridge, Southey, Thomas Arnold, William Whewell, Carlyle, 'Christopher North', etc. – in north-western England and southern Scotland. Braudel, in *The Mediterranean*, cites the resilience of small-scale democratic organisation in mountain areas (Braudel 1949). North-western England – an area of high literacy, local grammar schools with scholarships to the old universities, small 'statesmen' or independent farmers, and conservative populist politics – transformed this into a national paradigm: a reassuring combination of *Gemeinschaft* and civil society, far removed from the mighty social divide of the grain-producing regions in the south. This was productive both of a modernising drive – the destruction of internal barriers to transport and trade – and of a careful ethos of elite-led social reform (Annan 1958).

In a famous letter of 1828 to Eckermann, Goethe had classed the variety of the small German capitals as the glory of German culture, but what he had in mind was the elitist culture of the little courts. The interpretation of German romanticism which came from the English north-west was both more demotic and more nationalistic, perhaps comparable with the functions granted to 'poetic provinces' such as Swabia in the day of Friedrich Hölderlin and Ludwig Uhland (Greiner 1992). Aside from Carlyle's distinctive contribution, both Coleridge and Arnold drew deeply on German historical scholarship for their cyclic projections of history and the superiority they ascribed to 'cultivation' over 'civilisation' (Forbes 1952: 39). As much as Herder's linguistic, culturally grounded nationalism, such conservative British examples figured in the German response to Napoleonism, in which the smaller states – hitherto with quite distinctive foreign policies – came to be regarded as parts of the whole German community, even by 'minimal government' enthusiasts like Wilhelm von Humboldt. The *Zollverein* (German Customs Union) could fit into the conspectus of conservative modernisation in the tradition of Burke and Scott.

In the *Vormärz*, the pre-1848 liberal movement, local culture could still be compatible with the centralisation of the liberal, Protestant left, but in 1848 'particularism', the possession of the mainly Catholic right, was regarded as increasingly toxic, either because it was ultramontane, or associated with the Poles in Silesia (Eyck 1968). In contrast to England, the Protestant German 'mission' would mean a much greater direction by statute, the spread of education in the German language, the Luther Bible (which played a similar role to the King James Bible in Britain) and, in a more ecumenical sense, the renaissance in German literature in the late eighteenth century: Schiller, Goethe, Herder. Germany achieved, in comparison with Britain, an early and con-centrated cultural-political nationalism, with 'high' literature tending to be regarded as synonymous with 'German' literature and a peculiar sense of mission. This was to last. Despite their local presence in Brandenburg or Lubeck, Fontane or Mann are 'German' writers in a sense that Hardy is never wholly an 'English' writer; between such and *Mundartschriftstellern* (dialect writers) is a great gap fixed.

The power of German uniformity: bureaucracy, military organ-isation, religious establishment, and after 1870 an imperial ethos, was vast. Perhaps all the stronger because of the existence of a more exposed German elite in the Habsburg Empire. There were statues of Goethe and Schiller, Bismarck and Emperor Wilhelm I throughout the country; the programme of the student societies at the universities was pan-German; to the Lutheran Church 'obedience to the state was a divinely ordained command' and military service was a universal experience of German youth (Stern 1987: 183).

In Germany, political decentralisation was countered by such attempts at cultural unity; in France, despite the Jacobin tradition, nationality was challenged by a powerful provincial culture. Paradoxically, the drastic extension of French culture after 1870 achieved by conscription, education and the improvement of communications was also accom-panied by the rise of provincial literary movements – Renan and the Breton revival, Mistral and Provençal. On the left, the Commune's attempt at municipal self-government laid the foundations of the regional geographical and historical studies of such as Elisée Reclus and Vidal de la Blache, which had become an orthodoxy by the early 1900s. On the right, the revived appeal of the provincialism of Maurice

Barrès and his right-wing *confrères* was a response to German military success (Meller 1990: 38f.; Weber 1991: 226f.).

PRINT-CAPITALISM AND CIVICS

The great powers dictated the structure of nineteenth-century political evolution and within them 'progressive opinion' regarded regionalism as a conservative distortion. 'National liberal' historians of the Heinrich von Treitschke sort discounted it, and stigmatised unexciting Italian urban republics or German imperial free cities as decadent, while accepting more-or-less crazy militarists and racists as 'natural' (Wallas 1914: 78). Regionalism as a form of political organisation risked, on the eve of the First World War, being ridiculed into 'Balkanisation' – although this miniaturised and malignant version of Bismarckian national egoism falsified any proper comprehension of it.

The more benign notion of the region as a culturally satisfying division of a national community again seems to originate in Britain, where the print-capitalism mechanism was most developed. It began as an essentially literary projection: the Yorkshire of the Brontës, vividly summed up in the first chapters of Mrs Gaskell's *Life of Charlotte Brontë* (1857), soon became a tourist pilgrimage; so too did Thomas Hardy's Dorset. Behind both, perhaps, stands another 'north-western' figure, John Ruskin, with his combination of 'civic virtue' – crystallised in his version of Venetian civilisation, but owing a lot to Carlyle – and downright reactionary anti-modernism.

This metropolitan exploitation mirrored native growths, such as Hartley's *Clock Almanacks* in Wakefield or the dialect poetry of William Barnes, which were in part the result of an 'international' development of phonetic shorthand in the 1830s (Salveson 1990). This regionalism was not, William Donaldson has argued in his remarkable work *Popular Literature in Victorian Scotland*, a flight into nostalgia. The vernacular literature of the Scottish north-east, the district around Aberdeen which was famed for its high quality of educational achievement and European contacts, attained levels comparable with the highest levels of European realism (Donaldson 1986: 124). Similar arguments were being made at the time for Nynorsk in Norway, Icelandic and Finnish, at a time when, in the greater European states, specific dialects – Tuscan, Langue d'Oeil, Hochdeutsch – were being granted official status.

But, in Britain, the political dimension was still missing. Engels, for example, was conscious of Manchester, in which he lived for some thirty years, not as a regional capital, but more as a sort of internationalised paradigm of the social alienation of capitalist industry (Briggs 1963, 1968: 111f.). Effective 'regionalism' presupposed an interventionist nation-state *and* a local bourgeoisie prepared to remain local. Unlikely among the beneficiaries of the 1832 Reform Act, whom the Empire and the public schools rapidly locked into a 'British' identity, this became more of a possibility later in the century (Wiener 1981: 16–22). A more radical, democratic mode was apparent in the 1900s in schemes like that of H.G. Wells for a 'new heptarchy' of regional councils controlling 'appropriate areas of government' (Wells 1908: 274).

In at least some British cities, this revival of culture came close to rivalling anything on the continent. The Glasgow of the 'Glasgow Boys', of the architects Rennie Mackintosh and Burnet, of Alfred Wareing's repertory theatre, the Orpheus Choir and the Independent Labour Party is most often cited, but 'New Liberal' Manchester fielded, before the First World War, C.P. Scott and his remarkable team at the *Manchester Guardian*, Ernest Rutherford, Chaim Weizmann, Samuel Alexander and R.H. Tawney at the University, the Gaiety Theatre, the plays of Stanley Houghton and Harold Brighouse, the novels of F.C. Montague and the early artistic career of L.S. Lowry. Even in the slump, Manchester culture was still lively between the wars, producing besides Beecham and Barbirolli, the novels of Howard Spring, and much of the political theatre movement. Joan Littlewood, Ewan MacColl and Sidney Bernstein started out from a town whose cosmopolitanism was expressed in the presence at its university of two of the greatest historians of the day – Sir Lewis Namier and A.J.P. Taylor (Middlemass 1965: 17–31; Clarke 1971).

Such local impulses issued in Sir Ernest Simon's 1940 manifesto *The Smaller Democracies of Europe* (Simon was a former Lord Mayor and leading Liberal.) During the First World War they already intersected with 'reconstruction' and the infant social sciences, leading to such a 'regionalist' manifesto as Fawcett's *The Provinces of England* (1921), which divided Britain into the spheres of interest of eight conurbations. The 'city-region' concept was essentially one aspect of the transatlantic migration of Scottish civic consciousness during the nineteenth century. Thomas Chalmers' *Christian and Civic Economy of Great Towns* (1821–6) influenced the Charity Organisation Society and Arnold Toynbee and through him, the university settlement movement, which rapidly developed on both sides of the Atlantic, becoming transformed into the American 'urban movement'.

With urbanisation in 1900 developing at roughly the same pace as in the United States, 'civics' became a concept central to the ordering of industrial society. This took on the democratic structure of 'progressivism' in the USA, the great city being seen as a source of opportunities as well as problems. In Britain its ideology was firmly anchored in the administrative and not-particularly-democratic approach of the Christian Socialists, the Positivists and the Charity Organisation Society, and contained a strongly anti-urban element, which went right back to the 'Lake District', through the influence of Ruskin on Octavia Hill, one of the founders in 1896 of the National Trust. In 1990 this 'voluntary' body, with a membership of more than two million, an area of action which includes all of the United Kingdom save Scotland, and assets of over £1 billion, has no European parallel.

The evolution of an informal, print-capitalism-led regionalism was frustrated on the continent not only because the formation of 'national' institutions preceded urbanisation. Nationality, and the political balances which underpinned it, had received a salutary check at its moment of triumph, with the Franco-Prussian War being rapidly followed by the Paris Commune of 1871 and the agricultural crisis of 1873. These events concentrated the attention of the military-bourgeois elites of the European states on retaining the peasantry on the land as sound conscripts and conservative voters, by tariffs designed to protect agriculture, along with credit banks, co-operatives, better roads and light railways. This both responded to populist ethnic and peasant movements and also contributed much of their culture – tidied-up national costumes, communal ceremonies, folk songs, regiments with local traditions. Thus, ironically, the state increasingly took over civic culture from the city in the early years of the twentieth century, a development accelerated by preparations for war, by the war itself, and subsequent economic depression. Just when the city-region was emerging as an intellectual framework marrying civics and space, the Versailles settlement would give a further lease of life to the ethnic-defensive ideal of nationalism.

3   Regional elites and regional culture

DRAMATIS PERSONAE

I live 70 miles from Switzerland, visit fairly frequently, receive Swiss television, and I can think of precisely three rather random Swiss politicians: Bonvin, Niggli and Kopp. I don't think I'm alone. Small-scale politics means small-scale careers. So if certain actors – classes and status groups – dominated regional development and determined the course that it took, they tend to remain opaque when viewed at a distance. Most people in Europe – in the late nineteenth century 80 per cent of the European population were subjects of the six great powers – more or less enthusiastically acquiesced in large-scale nationalism of a militarised and centralised type in part because national leaders (Napoleon, Cavour, Garibaldi, Bismarck) were projected on an over-human scale. But need this have been the case?

The explanation lies in the history of the European *bourgeois*. In his influential exploration of the nature of political 'hegemony', the Italian Marxist Antonio Gramsci drew on the 'elitist' critique of Marxism by Croce, Mosca and Pareto to stress the important role of the intelligentsia – which he divided into the 'organic' and the 'traditional' – in fusing economic base to politico-cultural superstructure (Gramsci 1971: 18). Within the 'civic' community, the stress must be on the 'organic' intelligentsia of capitalism. The 'traditional' intelligentsia of literati, priests and lawyers had a role to play, for sure, but they were paradoxically less rooted. They could go on being an intelligentsia in exile or in a 'cultural capital' which wasn't in their own country, like the Welsh in London, where Iolo Morganwg revived the Druidic *Gorsedd* on Primrose Hill. The Balts organised their independence movement from St Petersburg; the Czechs and Poles from Vienna; the Russian radicals from Switzerland. Yet the bourgeoisie, in their civic as well as economic role, their relation to patterns of international trade, became indispensable to the nationalism of the nineteenth century and the bureaucratic structures which it brought (Ludwig 1991; Williams 1985: 162).

THE COMMERCIAL BOURGEOISIE

Was the capture of the commercial bourgeoisie by nationalism inevitable? Great urban centres tended to be cosmopolitan, and if a political unit had several of them, or was in Stein Rokkan's term *polycephalous*, its organisation would also tend to be federalist or decentralised (Rokkan 1980: 192). Classic cases are the Hanse, whose constituent towns stretched from Trier to Tallinn, or Venice, and following them the seventeenth-century Netherlands: seven loosely linked provinces (severed by the sea and the Rhine delta) whose identity, according to Simon Schama, was conferred as much by the conflict between their trade and their religion as by their internal organisation (Schama 1987; Holton 1986).

The Habsburg Empire, the victim of Cavour and Bismarck, was nothing if not polycephalous. Even when Germans were 90 per cent of the population of Vienna, there were vociferous communities of Czechs, Poles, Hungarians and Jews. Prague – the city of Kafka and Rilke – was a major centre of German culture, although Germans were only 6 per cent of its population. In another example of the endangered species, 50 per cent of the investment of the Ottoman Empire in 1914 was in the hands of Greek Orthodox Christians (Kazamias 1991: 353). In Imperial Russia, polycephalous but far from democratic, St Petersburg had German and Swedish elites; London had, at least momentarily, Lenin and Stalin. It and Paris were packed with minorities, often influential. Conversely, even at the height of the nationalist epoch, local trading elites survived, very often with complex international connections. The financiers, merchants, shipowners of the North Sea ports and their economic hinterland – German merchant bankers who had flitted from the Hanse towns to London, German cotton and wool magnates in Manchester and Bradford, the fisheries bosses of Aberdeen and Hull – maintained an identity which lasted until the First World War. Scots names – Christies, Crichtons, Finlaysons – were frequently to be encountered in Scandinavia and on the shores of the Baltic. Immanuel Kant, incidentally a pioneer of human geography at the University of Königsberg, prided himself on his Forfarshire grandfather (Ashton 1986).

Did the ideology of national liberation induce ethnic exclusiveness? Jacobin chauvinism in France certainly excluded federalism from the remit of the National Assembly in 1848, but the Germans initially favoured a multi-ethnic federalism (Eyck 1968). In Italy, Vincenzo Gioberti argued for a confederation of constitutional states under the headship of the 'liberal' Pope Pius IX, and after a brief, absurd and almost bloodless civil war the multi-ethnic Swiss Confederation, along American lines, was confirmed. But there *is* a shift around 1848. The pluralism of the United States of America, earlier appreciated by Europeans who pointed to the contributions of their emigrants, seems to wilt. A bourgeoisie distrustful of mass politics distanced itself from Jacksonian democracy. It read de Tocqueville – himself a decentralist – and took to heart his picture of its anti-intellectual workings in his *Democracy in America* (1835). The threat of a militant proletariat, inflamed by cyclical unemployment, didn't help. Not everyone had de Tocqueville's young British disciples' faith, in *Essays on Reform* (1867), in a prehensile landed aristocracy as a brake on democracy (Harvie 1976: 157). Technology, on the other hand, offered opportunistic national elites the chance to achieve rapid unification at someone else's expense; and the United States demonstrated in the Civil War that violence was equally attractive to a democracy. In these circumstances a *politique* bourgeoisie explored alliances with the old order; the cosmopolitanism and shifting population of the towns became a menace to be disciplined, suppressed, and otherwise kept under, if necessary by stressing linkages to the countryside and its healthy, credulous peasantry (Craig 1991: 203ff.).

The attraction of economic nationalism varied inversely with the strength of free trade principles. Where subsidy, cartels and protection were important – as became increasingly the case – civic elites either declined or sidled into the lobbies of the national legislature (Borchardt 1973: 138). This did not happen in Denmark, with its agricultural exports, nor in Belgium and Holland with their huge entrepôt trade, nor in Switzerland with its tourism and transit traffic. The trading bourgeoisie in such places counted on international relationships and would be keener to reach an accommodation with its resident proletariat, than link up with the *ancien régime* (Tamse 1985). Bourgeois orientation also depended on technology, communications and the sort of politics on offer. Export- or military-oriented capital goods industries, steam-driven, increased the influence of the nation-state; electricity and the internal combustion engine later loosened such constraints. Industry could then cluster round the market of the metropolis (as with London in the inter-war years) or migrate to regions of abundant manpower but few mineral resources (as with southern Germany after 1945).

The nation-state frustrated regionalism but, as it intervened more in the economy, promoted 'regionalisation'. The Keynesian interventionist state coped with structural change by supplementing personal and participative rights with welfare rights, encouraging regional planning aimed at creating local markets for consumer goods and services, and decentralising its own organisation. New communications techniques reinforced this: radio and later television had to be organised regionally because of its limited transmission technology; cinema introduced a new cosmopolitan culture which weakened national loyalties. As for the potency of local institutions: where they were weak – as in Britain – the bourgeoisie were swift to decouple. Businessmen on Lancashire County Council fell from 45.7 per cent in 1889, to 21.4 per cent in 1928 and only 2.4 per cent in 1970 (Marshall 1977: 57, 221). Where they were strong – and in post-1945 Germany, particularism helpfully coalesced with the Allied desire for a weak central power – they attracted business support (Boelcke 1987: 454ff.).

THE STATE AND ITS INSTITUTIONS

Friedrich List, the advocate of industrialisation through protection, proposed an all-German railway system in 1839. This was promptly seconded by the future Field Marshal von Moltke. Armies and railways, organised on national lines, had sharply 'nationalising' effects on insecure bourgeoisies. Indeed, they advanced in parallel, as the use of railways as the major means of mobilisation was fixed in the military mind after the revolutions of 1848. From then until the First World War the major European states followed Prussia and laid their railways out essentially for military purposes, not just to speed troops to the frontiers but to connect up all the regional centres of mobilisation. This affected secular transport provision. Ships, even steamships, were reasonably cheap – which was why a small country like Norway had so many of them. All you needed was hull, engines, crew – and you could buy them second-hand. Railways – because of land purchase – were hugely expensive and by no means profitable (Pratt 1915: 8).

This enormous outlay had somehow to be financed. States encouraged freight traffic and if necessary subsidised it, with the result that the self-governing mercantile cities were threatened. When Mecklenburg, for example, entered the *Zollverein* in 1868, the commerce of its chief port, the *Hansestadt* of Rostock, collapsed, since grain was railed to Berlin instead of exported. The fall of Thomas Mann's Buddenbrook family was linked to Lubeck's decline as railways linked Prussia with the North Sea ports of Bremen and Hamburg. For other ports, becoming a railway or trade fair centre, securing lines into the hinterland, became of crucial importance. In Austria, Trieste was only enabled to compete with Genoa as an outlet for German goods when the state built the Tauernbahn in the 1900s. The Hungarians ignored it and built a line to their own port at Fiume (Rijeka). In all these cases, what mattered were the links built up with the state authorities (Robbins 1970).

Conscript armies had a similar, centralising effect. This is still visible today in Spain, where military rule lasted until 1975, and the army is still deeply hostile to decentralisation (Gallagher 1991: 122). Following the success of Prussia, in late-nineteenth-century Europe a uniform structure of military governorships and mobilisation centres either supplemented the pattern of prefectorial government or was imposed on existing structures. Smaller states were late to adopt the conscription package: Holland only in 1901, Belgium in 1906. The Jacobin ethos of the 'citizen in arms' forged in the wars of revolutionary and Napoleonic France was not a foregone conclusion (Tamse 1985: 418–19).

Militarism boosted national identity almost as a function of the 'military participation ratio', which related the spread of 'demotic' ideology to the intensity of the conflict. It was a violent complement to Mazzinian nationalism, taking as axiomatic the relation between patriotism and fighting. Yet the mercenary spirit continued, and had an ambiguous influence on the growth, or survival, of 'pre-modern' areas which had a vested interest in the supply of soldiers, such as Ireland or Croatia. Even democracies regarded certain regions as embodying the military and patriotic virtues: they integrated them through military participation but also used them as a counterweight to the urban 'core'. East Prussia, Spanish Galicia, Brittany, Ireland and the Scottish highlands are examples. This specialisation was, however, risky. Either their economic underdevelopment meant that young men from such areas were more likely to be conscripted, and thus to die, increasing the likelihood of regional disaffection, or they were identified by urban radicals, or repressed groups, as centres of reaction (Janowitz 1957, 1968: 352).

The 'Swiss model' carried on the Machiavellian civic tradition, converting the mercenary spirit into that of the militia. Jonathan Steinberg devotes most of his treatment of Swiss national identity to the role of the citizen army (Steinberg 1974). Pacific and non-militarist Britain also contributed. Perhaps the most 'British' moment of the nineteenth century was the Volunteer movement of 1859, with its scratch regiments of artisans, railwaymen and professional men, ranged against putative French aggressors – and incompetent British generals – after the Crimean War. The north of England was energetic; Friedrich Engels was an enthusiastic volunteer officer. There was above-average volunteering among the Scots, partly through their mercenary and militia traditions. Evangelical Christian 'missions' to city dwellers produced bodies like the Boys' Brigade and later the Scouts; these combined with the military traditions of 'backward' areas, such as the highlands, into a 'national' tradition which spanned urban life and imperial enthusiasm (Cunningham 1975: 46–7).

Bureaucracy. Alan Beith once offered a special subject on 'comparative bureaucracies' at Newcastle University. It sounded so boring than no one took it, and he got on with becoming MP for Berwick. Yet this was the pivot of Max Weber's study of political organisation – from charisma through tradition to bureaucracy (Page 1991: 13–32). Of the three main structures found in Europe, the traditional patterns were associated with particularism – and heterogeneity, as conservative national regimes often favoured devolving executive powers to local elites, saving the trouble of setting up salaried systems. In Britain, so James Bulpitt's 'central autonomy' thesis runs, this ensured that local elites took control of 'gas-and-water' politics and such economic policy as the government cared to have, leaving parliament to consider the 'high politics' of the services, foreign and imperial affairs. Hence an effective degree of regionalisation in fact existed, with executive action being delegated to counties and boroughs, which became – in a rather haphazard way – 'collectors of tasks from central government' (Bulpitt 1983; Marshall 1977: 27). In Scotland one might even talk of survivals of 'charisma' since the Kirk remained responsible for poor relief and education until the 1840s.

The more decentralised a state, the less uniform its bureaucracy. Britain thus had a smallish, non-industrial civil service – 16,000 in 1800, 40,000 in 1850, around a quarter of a million in 1914 – but a large variety of urban bureaucracies. Switzerland was even more heterogeneous, but elsewhere on the continent the preference was for a salaried bureaucracy extending deep into civil society, both on the *ci-devant* enlightened despot right and on the Jacobin left. In France, where there was no tradition of local democracy, and the mayors were subservient to the prefects as the local executive level of central government, the number of civil servants increased from 119,000 in 1830 to 776,000 in 1914 (Price 1990: 47–54). Yet, even in this highly centralised system, it was often in the prefect's interest to foster local identity – a literate press, theatres, intellectual salon society – in order to increase his reputation and consequently his clout in Paris (Machin 1977; Ashford 1982). In doing this, he started out with a big advantage over the local mayor. Even in the 1970s 'A post in a town hall, even in a big place like Toulouse, offers poor pay, worse prestige and limited prospects, and does not attract the bright graduates of ENA and other elite schools' (Ardagh 1979: 301).

The Germanic system, as reformed by Stein and Hardenberg in the early nineteenth century, was supposed to imitate the 'self-government' of the English, but in fact it had been for some time influenced by France. What emerged was a more liberal version of French authoritarianism, with the higher bureaucracy (trained humanistically in the normal universities), based in its county (Kreis) offices. This developed as a counterweight to the otherwise looser structure of the federal empire, by opening the prospect for bureaucrats of transfers from state to state (Schulze 1985: 207–10). Even today, in the Bundesrepublik, the lines between *Land* and *Land*, and between civil service and political career, remain remarkably blurred.

A common and systematic bureaucracy could be a neutral force, and in north Europe it usually was. In Scandinavia, both Denmark and Sweden – the dominant powers – developed and exported a bureaucracy after the German pattern, but this if anything assisted the marriages and divorces which they and their neighbours went through. The bureaucratic substructure met with general agreement as a factor which could control any 'extremist' popular politics, and concessions were made to moderate nationalism which kept this structure in being (Bjorn 1993; Endemann 1991: 97–120). Matters were other in Italy, where the elite of the backward south, deprived of a commercial future by free trade politics which ruined such industries as they had, moved into the politics and administration of the centralised state, until they made up a steady 60 per cent of the bureaucracy after 1945. 'By the 1980s,' Tom Gallagher writes, 'the north was coming to resemble an advanced economic periphery in a state directed from and staffed from the south' (Gallagher 1992: 472).

THE CLERGY

Religion is now regarded as much more problematic than it was, say, in the 1960s. Events throughout Europe and the Middle East have disproved simple assumptions about 'secularisation'. Right up to the 1890s, Europe was a believing continent. Although governmental attitudes to tolerance varied from country to country, the conservatives' will to impose uniformity conflicted with their need to retain a system of social discipline which, even if conducted in another tongue, was reliable. In the Duchy of Poznan, the Prussians had still to allow Polish in periods of religious instruction, just as in Wales the Society for the Propagation of Christian Knowledge transferred proselytism from

English to Welsh in the eighteenth century. The risk was, of course, that even this minimal support might fan linguistic nationalism into existence (Kerr 1992).

In France, Catholicism was the belief of 90 per cent of the population, though the governing elite was disproportionately Protestant, deistic or downright atheistic. Only after the 1900s, in the aftermath of the Dreyfus case, did a secular programme take effect, intensifying the struggles within the state. Catholicism tended to align with French provincialism, because it seemed diametrically opposed to Jacobin secularism, and politically inclined clergy made it a point of focus. Provincialism was also an aspect of the conservative nationalism of such as Count Gobineau in the 1840s, and the more radical variant of Maurice Barrès in the France of the Third Republic (Biddiss 1970: 70; Weber 1991: 226). The French right also had a profound effect on Irish and Welsh nationalism, in the first case through political Catholicism, the anti-English propaganda of Maude Gonne, and the influence of the Presentation Brothers, with their fiercely nationalist, anti-semitic propaganda, and in the second through an Anglican exaltation of local community over class politics (Foster 1988; Sherrington 1980).

In Germany, too, Catholicism stood for the rights of the states (such of them as were Catholic, at any rate) and the Polish minority against those of the imperial government in Berlin. This reached a climax during the *Kulturkampf* of 1870–9 when Bismarck and his National-Liberal allies pursued a policy of secularisation and the expulsion of monastic orders. Fearing conservative weakness in the face of the socialist threat, Bismarck called the campaign off, and by the end of the nineteenth century, clergy, gentry and military co-operated to protect provincial cultures. *Trachtenvereine* (peasant costume societies) date from the 1880s; they helped retain a 'peasant culture' of religious processions, fairs, and *Bauerntheater* – comic drama – even when participants were really dependent on industrial employment, railways and tourism. Successful in Catholic Bavaria, this however led to a competing cultural movement in Alsace, in a German-language but anti-Reich theatre (Wilkinson 1989; Bausinger 1983: 19–30). Catholicism's 'Europeanism' and provincial identity were underwritten by its comparatively peripatetic nature; the clergy had always journeyed to Rome, or to seminaries; the laity along traditional pilgrimage routes to Padua, Compostella or Kevelaer. In the Catholic equivalent to the Protestant 'revivalism' of the late nineteenth and twentieth centuries (from Moody and Sankey to Billy Graham), these were supplemented by new goals such as Lourdes, Knock or Medjugorci. Catholic social teaching strongly influenced both the 'Europeanism' of post-1945 Bavaria, which was enthusiastic about federalism where the rest of Germany was not, and the 'principle of subsidiarity' which broke from nowhere on the European scene after Maastricht (Dorondo 1992: 31–42).

Not surprisingly, stay-at-home Lutheranism proved more pliable to state intervention in religion, granted its inclination to acquiesce in such control. To Fritz Stern, the secularisation of the Lutheran Church in Wilhelmine Germany set the scene for its capitulation to Hitler (Stern 1987). On the other hand, the Lutheran Church claimed virtually total allegiance in all the Scandinavian countries, and was quite neutral in national issues. In Denmark, however, Nicholas Grundtvig's combination of revivalism and popular education was to have a distinctive impact on the rise of a popular and democratic nationalism, and be copied elsewhere in Scandinavia and in Wales. Much less salient on the continent – although not wholly absent – was the local elitism of nonconformist sects, such as the Unitarians or Quakers, who were so influential among the English provincial middle class; although pietism played rather a similar role in Protestant south Germany and Switzerland. In general, such groups were particularist, but even they proved susceptible to imperialism in the critical years of 1890 to 1914 (Kerr 1992).

THE SOCIALISTS

Sir Halford Mackinder, geo-politics expert and organiser of Oxford University extension, the establishment's answer to Patrick Geddes as a theorist of provincial restructuring, sat as Liberal Unionist MP for a Glasgow seat until 1922. In *Democratic Ideas and Reality* (Mackinder 1919), he noticed that in the election of 1918 the class politics and industrial self-government offered by the Soviet revolution cut completely across any local loyalties on the part of the red Clydesiders he was up against (Mackinder 1919: 264). If this was the case in an area in which Labour had always had a strong local identity, the weakness of regional reform elsewhere in Britain seems explicable enough.

Socialist 'utopianism' literally had a strong element of the 'no-place' to it. Moreover, the conservative, clerical, aspects of 'particularism' provoked much hostility from organised labour – for example in the controversy in the German SPD over the 'peasantry question': the small landholder being seen by the 'orthodox' wing as irrecoverably clericalist and conservative. 'Revisionists' such as Eduard Bernstein campaigned both to reclaim the class for radical politics, and to develop civic government into a progressive force along Fabian socialist lines. But they were by and large exceptional in Europe before 1914.

This wasn't surprising, for at a regional level, at least in Germany, it was difficult for socialists to hope for parliamentary power of any sort. In the Diets of Prussia and Saxony, a 'three-class' franchise was retained, and even strengthened, during the imperial period, while the Reich itself had an equal franchise. As a result, any Saxon socialist's political expectations would be focused on Berlin, not on Dresden. After the creation of the Weimar Republic, the socialist distrust of local oligarchies was reflected in the strongly interventionist powers vested in the Reich government, although in the event these were used *against* left-wing governments in the provinces (Bramke 1993).

Socialist distrust of provincialism was also evident in Belgium, where the industrialisation process was early and a powerful socialist movement, based on co-operatives, existed by the 1870s. This movement, however, was urban and Francophone, while the further direction of Belgian industrial growth involved the 'suburbanisation' of practically the whole country. Workers commuting by rail and by the 'Vicinal' (the network of steam tramways which the government built up after the 1880s) enabled industry, usually owned by Francophone Belgians, to spread into the relatively undeveloped Flemish-speaking provinces. The socialists were ill-adapted to proselytise among this new proletariat, and its 'class' resentment was instead directed against a French-speaking bourgeoisie by Catholic populist and Flemish nationalist politicians. As a result, the Belgian socialist movement peaked in the 1890s, and did not develop further until after the First World War. A similar development characterised the 'peasant-workers' of parts of southern Germany, who retained their smallholdings – and conservative politics – while working in factories (Strikwerda 1989: 82–96; Boelcke 1987).

Many of the best organised industrial workers were not urban. Miners – who dominated the pre-1918 British Labour party – were predominantly a rural population; as were many textile workers. They could show exemplary solidarity, and be strong Scottish or Welsh nationalists and/or internationalists, but they had little knowledge of or interest in the affairs of a wider community, as the Labour party found when it tried to interest them in more general urban reform (McKibbin 1974).

The one group of socialists who tried to go out from the municipal programme to establish a philosophy of localised socialism were the Fabians in Britain; but even they were constrained by the slow engagement of government in municipal reform. A major depression hit British cities in the year of Liberal triumph 1906, which brought an end to much construction work and ended the control of London by the Fabian-Liberal Progressive Party. In power, the Liberals were disappointing, even though their local government minister was the former Labour MP John Burns. It was the old Whigs, Lords Pentland and

Aberdeen, who were the patrons of Patrick Geddes. Even then the municipal socialist impulse was strong among the Scottish left: in Tom Johnston's and John Wheatley's schemes for municipal enterprise and housing construction, a regional rather than nationalist tradition was continued (Meller 1990: 131–7; Wood 1989: 34).

In a negative sense, local loyalties within the British Labour movement remain far fiercer than in Germany: it is unthinkable for the Labour party to send a front-bencher to head the Labour group in Newcastle (let alone Aberdeen), although this inter-regional movement of political talent has been frequent in the German SPD, from Weimar to the present. But in Germany, the enduring foundations of bureaucracy and educational and social relationships have been at once uniform *and* decentralised, while the fissures between the British nations and between province and metropolis in England, have gone deep and preserved ancient animosities.

The other left tradition was that of anarchism, which took its cue from the federal enthusiasms of the pre-1848 period as well as the infant socialist movement. Expressed most eloquently by the Russians Kropotkin and Bakunin, it argued for a Europe organised through associations of producers and cantonal governments. Politically, this tradition was most significant in Holland, Switzerland and Spain – countries which had always had a strong federalist tradition – but through Elisée Reclus, it also influenced French and British regional studies, notably those of Geddes and his disciples. The watchmakers of the Jura were particularly influential on Kropotkin. In the 1900s, a variant of this expressed its revolutionary potential as syndicalism, but the triumph of state socialism in Russia after 1917 again marginalised it (Kropotkin 1942: 32–3). His English disciple Herbert Read was, however, to be influential on Leopold Kohr's 'small state' concepts in the 1940s and 1950s.

TEACHING AND TRAINING

Public instruction was a battlefield of the Jacobin state and its opponents. In France, the local schoolmaster became the instrument of a centralised culture expressive of the dominant language. This was not, however, replicated in all centralising régimes, even authoritarian ones. They wanted to maintain the social discipline imparted by family and religion, and thus were prepared to tolerate instruction in the native tongue, as with the Poles or the Welsh. The Turkish Empire adopted a specifically religious structure of devolution whereby the Orthodox patriarch in Constantinople headed a Christian *millet* responsible for education. This Turkish imperial community for minority groups endured for over 400 years, providing a reasonable degree of toleration (Kazamias 1991: 344–51).

If the advance of commerce put the Turks on the defensive, as their subjects demanded a more secular curriculum, secondary and tertiary education was sensitive throughout Europe. Under Napoleon, the French universities were reorganised into a centrally structured system of faculties, intended to supply the teachers and lawyers for the secular state. Along with this went, in France, the systematic dismantling of the local restrictions on labour organisation and training which contradicted the operations of a free market. None the less, the bourgeois order also required two further things: the development of technical instruction and the maintenance of social discipline through religious instruction. In this – as in the universities – the Jacobin pattern was far from efficient (Anderson 1975).

In Germany, the Jacobin pattern was in part emulated, with the closure in the 1880s of several of the older universities (Mainz, Cologne, Erfurt, for example) and the creation, by the monarchs of Prussia and Bavaria, of three large new universities at Bonn, Berlin and Munich. Much more than the highly stylised teaching of the French universities, these were devoted to the intellectual goals of *Lehrfreiheit* (freedom to choose what to teach) and *Lernfreiheit* (freedom to learn), and acted as beacons of academic reform throughout Europe (Arnold 1868). But they also had the effect of overshadowing the traditional universities of the smaller states. The cultural multiplicity that Goethe had commended to Eckermann was already going into eclipse, to be replaced by a type of territorial representation through the nationalistic *Burschenschaften* (student corporations) – Rhenania, Suevia, Allemania, and so on – of large and increasingly conservative universities. This came to a symbolic climax in the 1890s with the campaign to build above every German university town a 'Bismarck Tower' to commemorate the architect of German unity. Not surprisingly, the universities had by 1933 advanced further towards extreme nationalism than any other German institution.

In contrast to this, the regional authorities began, from the middle of the nineteenth century, to rebuild the structures of industrial and craft training in ways which reinforced the self-confidence of the *Mittelstand* – the small masters and retailers who felt themselves threatened by the onslaught of market forces. Statutory Chambers of Commerce and Handcrafts were allowed to govern entry into skilled trades and retailing, and strict trading hours were enforced, as those concerned were seen as an element of stability to be deployed against the socialist movement. The relatively unideological training so provided meant that their institutions survived the upheavals of 1933–45 and were a major element in the reassertion of the power of the local bourgeoisie in German federalism. Even today, the network of responsibilities centred on education – research, technology transfer, culture – remains the greatest concentration of authority in the German *Länder* (Schröder 1991; Edwards 1978: 188).

THE INTELLECTUALS

The clergy had always, in the pre-revolutionary state, been the supplier of ideology to the peasant masses, presiding over the fairs and rituals which mediated a localised popular culture. In the course of the eighteenth century, however, its function began to change, with secular-isation, the growth of scepticism and a commercial order in rural society. Given a weak legislature, the clergy became the prototype of the historians and ideologues who were to dominate intellectual life. Principal Robertson, Adam Ferguson and the Scottish Moderates were a leading example of this transition, and had a direct effect on continental evolution through their influence on French secular cen-tralists such as Guizot and Cousin (Davie 1961). Elsewhere the clergy became the protectors of a more specific ethnic identity, both in reaction to the Jacobin challenge, as in Spain, or in an attempt to emulate it, as in Ireland.

Print-capitalism, the rise of the novel, and secularism, gradually switched the focus of activity from the church to the universities and the urban communities, and the work of the historian and the philologist began to take effect. The challenge of print assaulted the local dialects which predominated throughout Europe, by selecting one (often arbi-trarily) as the 'pure' language, to be confirmed through the compilation of dictionaries and grammars. In the Czech districts of Bohemia, the shift from religion – a weak ethnic unifying factor, because Catholicism had been imposed on the country in the seventeenth century – to history and linguistic nationalism marked the early years of the nineteenth century. Czech identity reflected a 'dominant' historical nationality, albeit one which had to take its chance among the competitor *ethnies* of the Habsburg Empire. It benefited, to some extent, from patronage from the government in Vienna, eager to use it as a counterweight to German liberals; such patronage from large, autocratic units could always elevate a regional into a contestant nationalist movement (Taylor 1941, 1976: 33).

Yet, in the epoch of print-capitalism, even a nationalist agenda required a regional frame. A popular literature, of the sort which the novel offered, had to have a *mise-en-scène* to which its readers could relate. The problem of novels or poems with a political agenda was that if they were rendered purely in terms of 'high politics', then no ordinary reader could relate to them at all. They had to be grounded, as Carlyle wrote of Walter Scott, in the actions and feelings of 'real people', and these were to be encountered in the more intimate environment of the region, or a particular occupation. Scott consciously aimed to achieve this by basing each of his Waverley novels in a specific region of Scotland – *The Heart of Midlothian* in Edinburgh, *Rob Roy* in Glasgow and the Trossachs, *The Pirate* in the Orkneys, and so on. In England, on the other hand, the activities of politics, religion and, education, themselves became types of provinces: smaller, specialised worlds with their own personal relations, crowd scenes and melodramas (Harvie 1991; Léclaire 1954).

Russia seems to be the exception which proves the rule. The great novels of that sequence from Gogol to Gorki seem peculiarly ideal-typical in the purity of their moral debate, the confrontation of 'Moscow' and the province, the absence of regional contaminations. Elsewhere, as the tide of urbanisation seemed unstoppable, the region or the smaller town modulated into a type of compensatory, conservative community. Here it performed a vicarious activity of socialisation. This was found at its most sophisticated in Britain, with the rise of the 'Kailyard school' of rural (and often clerical) moralists in Scotland, and the 'educational' portrayal of Cornwall in the work of Sir Arthur Quiller-Couch, who also occupied the 'strategic' chair of English literature at Cambridge (Ehrlich 1988).

The 'vanishing' province was utilised by continental novelists, but not as reassuringly. Theodor Fontane, raised on Scott, balanced a sort of horrified fascination with the growth of Berlin against the tranquillity of the neighbouring Mark Brandenburg, but with Thomas Mann's elegy on the Lübeck *Patrizier* in *Buddenbrooks*, a sense of the alienation of what Graham Wallas called 'the great society' supervened. With a much sharper message, the French radical nationalist Maurice Barrès, moving from left to right, set the decencies of Lorraine against the decadence of the metropolis in *Les Déracinés* (Weber 1991: 226). At the other extreme, was the sense of an alienated, totalitarian power in Franz Kafka a product of his own mental state? Or was it the product of the problems of a prosperous Jewry in a cosmopolitan city co-existing with an authoritarian imperialism? Perhaps Jewishness, with its urban identity and sense of the Law, was less susceptible to nationalism and more mindful of the civic. The berater *par excellence* of Viennese society was Karl Kraus, and certainly the modernist novel's greatest triumph involved a Jew in a meticulously realised provincial city: James Joyce's *Ulysses* (Janik and Toulmin 1973: 266–8).

MASS CULTURE

Some of the industrial epoch's influences on the spread – or limitation – of provincial culture were less portentous. Sport had been claimed by Adam Ferguson as a precursor of William James's 'moral equivalent of war' and its pre-industrial apparitions – folk-football, *cnapan* in Wales, *barette* in France – were, along with bound-beating ceremonies, a projection of localism. The transformation of such games from ritual to competition in the second half of the nineteenth century was another innovation of English 'informal self-government', closely bound up with notions of civic betterment (Ferguson 1767, 1966: 42–50; Meller 1976). Football, in its increasingly commercial post-1880 mode, reflected the impact of national news media and transport facilities. The Scottish and English leagues, organised in the 1870s, might have given way to a single 'British' league had they been organised – like most European countries – in the 1890s, when the rail network was better developed. Distinctive types of sports grew more densely in the regions of the British Isles than was the case in Europe: working-class rugby union in Wales and the Scottish borders; professional rugby league in Lancashire and Yorkshire, 'Gaelic' games in Catholic Ireland (Jarvie and Walker 1993). A sharp divide persisted between the 'competitive' ethic of the Protestant north – expressed through the nineteenth-century suppression of 'cruel sports' as well as encouragement of team games – and the survival of local rituals, frequently involving brutal, quasi-sacrificial sports – bull-fighting, the Pamplona bull-run, the Sienese *palio* – in the Mediterranean countries. But the advantage in future development rested with the north.

In the early 1900s, and linked to sports coverage, the mass-circulation press increasingly made its presence felt, at the cost of the collaborative ethos of the local weeklies. Its diet of scandal, crime and (usually) extreme nationalism, pioneered in France and Britain, encouraged cognate entertainments – popular comedy and music or crime fiction – as yet less subject to historical analysis. These could be national or regional. Why, for example, are German printed *Krimis* (crime stories) stubbornly Anglo-Saxon, but TV detectives provincial? Elsewhere the *roman policier* seems, in the hands of the Belgian Georges Simenon, the Anglo-Dutch Nicholas Freeling, and the Scots-Irish William MacIlvanney, to provide a 'strangers' guide' to provincial towns, as much as the products of Eugène Sue and Conan Doyle did for Paris and London.

Mass tourism is equally unexplored. Probably neutral in its effects? The *Grillplätze* (suntan factories) of the Adriatic or the Costa Brava failed to induce any alteration in the behaviour of either their visitors or the mores of the 'host' society – as the Jugoslav civil war demonstrated. Nor (save in Italy) did more than a fraction of 'sightseeing' visitors penetrate beyond the capital cities. The semi-affluent, middle-class tourist, on the other hand, often indulged in spectacular transfers of loyalty, particularly from England and Germany to Tuscany and the Dordogne. Linked to this was the rise of 'serious cooking' in the hands of Elizabeth David, Wolfram Siebeck and Jane Grigson. 'International' cuisine had hitherto been French, expensive, and spread by diplomats; now it was peasant-derived and spread by academics. The late Elizabeth David has been credited with 'Europeanising' the English more than any politician by changing their tastes. With good reason.

A NATIONALIST AGENDA

Nationalism, and the technology and forms of organisation its leaders selected, generally preceded industrialisation. Napoleonic France was followed by the Frankfurt parliament whose federal and multi-ethnic intentions rapidly narrowed into German centralism, for 'left' as much as 'right' reasons. There were exceptions to this trend: the Low Countries and Scandinavia, but these were on a small scale. This 'national mobilisation' charted out the institutional field for other types of conflict, industrial or religious. The major European powers could take heart from the massive deployment of force by central governments against the insurgency in Southern Italy, 1861–5, and the Paris Commune of 1871.

Elsewhere, conservative interventionism aimed at populist solidarity through welfare measures and opposition to 'non-national' groups – demonstrated by anti-semitic politicians such as Pastor Stöcker in Berlin and Mayor Lueger in Vienna. Such issues infiltrated themselves into urban life in Wilhelmine Germany. On balance, however, a British regionalist such as Patrick Geddes was greatly impressed by the new city as a force for a revived regional politics, whether in imperial Germany or in the USA of the 'progressive' era. Towards the end of the First World War it seemed for a time as if the predictions in Oswald Spengler's *Decline of the West* would be realised, and that the future would lie with the smaller states.

4 Regions in the epoch of the nation-state

THE ETHNIC EPOCH

The creation of functioning federal or semi-federal structures in all the major European states, with the exception of Britain, has been the work of the last forty years, and outside Germany effectively of the last twenty years. Why have these been successful, where earlier attempts either failed, or were not considered important?

In terms of interpretation, one consequence of our foreshortened historical perspective is that it has been evicted from the inputs of the other social sciences. Regional culture, education and local government, once made subordinate to linguistic nationalism, social security and military requirements, slipped away not only from *realpolitik* but from the academic study of politics. 'It is very difficult to speak of "local" industrial policy when the French social sciences deny the reality of the locality', comments L.H. Schlenker, describing the 'regionalisation' programme of Mitterrand (Schlenker 1987: 267–72). An astonishing statement about the country that, more than any other, fostered the geography and history of regional studies through Reclus, Vidal de la Blache and Braudel. Yet this registers the academic apartheid which obtains in this area, where the procedures of administrative analysis are so remote from those of cultural studies.

Why is this? To many, it was a surprise to be told by Eugen Weber about the regionality of Third Republic France. Under assault from school, railway and conscription, the self-identity of the provinces chopped up into prefect-run *départements* was closer, ironically, to that described by Braudel in the seventeenth century, than to the ambitious post-1981 regions (Weber 1979; Braudel 1988). How much was this 'disremembering' due to a 'Jacobin' schoolbook history which interrogated the regional past for evidence of uniform reaction to the great discontinuities of national history, rather than the diversity which stemmed from the constitution of the region? As Jean-Paul Sartre wrote in his 1970 essay on the Burgos trials of Basque separatists:

> [French children are taught that the history of France consists in the unification of all 'our' provinces, begun by the Kings, carried on by the French Revolution and completed in the nineteenth century. When I was at school I was taught to be proud of this. The attainment of national unity, once it had been achieved, explained the perfection of our language and the universality of our culture. Whatever our political goals, this was beyond challenge. On this point, socialists and communists were at one with conservatives./
>
> (Sartre 1971: 3)

While sympathetic to the revolutionary potential of such movements, Sartre ended pessimistic about France itself: 'For there exists a Basque people and a Breton people, but Jacobinism and industrialisation have liquidated our people, today there are only French masses' (Sartre 1971: 21).

THE IDEOLOGIES OF REGIONALISM

The historian has got to excavate for non-mainstream factors, approaches invoked only when events make accepted sequences irrelevant. Obviously, a history predicated on the catastrophes of the two world wars highlights the military and diplomacy, the 'high politics' of national governments and parliaments. In this unfavourable situation, which factors conserved local identity, and which obscured it?

Social action had its 'unanticipated consequences': trading relationships were disrupted by the railway, that great instrument of national economics, but the consciousness of port towns survived. The basins of industrial production developed distinctive blends of localism, capitalism and socialism. International commercial law and non-national cultural/political affiliations (trade, religion, socialism) created some degree of common identity across formal frontiers. Part of this 'alternative history' is, however, the result of ideology: the evolution of regionalism from bogeyman 'particularism' to a rational goal. What factors influenced this, and where should we enquire after them? If Jacobinism conflated the ethnic and the military, where did the dynamic of shared economic interests survive? What happened to the Machiavellian ideal of 'civic virtue' inhering in local government?

To start with the last. Eugenio Biagini has seen a localist tradition enduring within the popular politics of working-class intellectuals, for example in the Paris Commune of 1871 and the support of it by British radicals. That this was more communitarian than socialist is also shown by their enthusiasm for Switzerland (Biagini 1992: 12, 62–9). Decentralism, however, was not confined to the left. In the 1840s, Alexis de Tocqueville favoured a re-provincialised France, although he was unable to do anything about it while he was Foreign Minister in the government of 1849. Pierre-Auguste de Gobineau, his Political Secretary, founded the *Revue Provincielle* to press for this, although he became better known for his 'scientific' racialism. Catholic conservatives followed Frédéric Le Play in positing regionalism as an alternative to class politics and secular nationalism, which could also lead to the Catholic international ideal of a continuing Christendom. This was represented in Britain by James Monteith and David Urquhart (also the great proponent of popular involvement in foreign policy) and later on by G.K. Chesterton and, in Wales, Saunders Lewis (Biddiss 1970: 70–3; Aspinwall 1982: 57–70).

On the left, communists, abandoning international revolution for 'socialism in one country' surrounded Stalin's Russia by 'popular fronts' which existed to conserve 'progressive' national traditions. Their victims were not only Trotskyists, but the anarchist tradition out of which Kropotkin's friend Elisée Reclus, an ex-Communard, laid the foundations of regional geography. From this was created both the 'from the ground up' history of the *Annales* school, and the regionalism of Patrick Geddes and his followers (Meller 1990: 38, 124).

Quasi-anarchist initiatives marked the politics of the 1900s: pluralism expressed in the 'corporate' identity of churches and trade unions, syndicalism and guild socialism, federalism. But federal theorists – Freeman, Lorimer, Bryce, the young Laski – were overshadowed by the cataclysm of 1914, the rejection of multinationality at Versailles, even the failure of Versailles itself. Prophets of self-government and 'international public right', such as Gladstone, were unfathomable to a centralised English elite which created its own economics and class-based 'behaviourist' political analysis. Even regional geography, which underlay many of the proposals of planners and politicians, gave way in the 1950s to the 'quantitative revolution' of exploring functional structures on a comparative basis and testing appropriate – Marxian or anti-Marxian – models. To investigate those analysts of urban and industrial society, who argued for smaller units of organisation is (at least for historians) a venture into near-unexplored territory.

INTERNATIONAL LAW AND THE SCOTTISH TRADITION

'Now we can discuss the Breton question', said the Breton nationalist Morvan Lebesque on hearing of Hiroshima. The military rationale of the nation-state, as well as checking regional development, sidelined the ideas for international order, involving peacekeeping measures in a disarmed Europe, first raised by Henry IV of France in the seventeenth century and revived by Leibniz, Rousseau and Kant in the eighteenth century. The moralistic nationalism of Mazzini believed that, once national liberation had been achieved, national 'missions' would realise themselves in spontaneous international collaboration. Instead, national *realpolitik* threatened clashes on a scale that could shatter even the largest units.

In this context, international law was usually seen as a form of damage limitation, enforcing rules of war or arbitration procedures. In the 1860s, these produced Leber's military code in the American Civil War, and the Alabama arbitration case which followed it (Best 1980). But other thinkers, notably from smaller European nations – Scotland, Switzerland and Holland – envisaged international bodies that were legislative rather than judicial. The Swiss-German jurist J.K. Bluntschli proposed a European confederation in his *Europa als Staatenbund* (1871), but it was German-dominated and heavily armed. The response of his colleague James Lorimer, of Edinburgh University, in his *The Institutes of the Law of Nations* (Lorimer 1884), was much more radical: a scheme for a United States of Europe, with an elected legislature. Lorimer was a disarmer and liberal: in what Bluntschli called his 'international republic', he worked out in some detail 'how to find international equivalents for the factors known to national law as legislation, jurisdiction and execution' (Lorimer 1884: 186).

Lorimer proposed a Senate and a Chamber of Deputies. The six great powers – Britain, France, Austria, Italy, Russia and Germany – would each get five life Senators and fifteen elected Deputies; the smaller countries a lesser number. A fifteen-man ministry, five of whom would be Senators and which would have one representative of each great power, would be balanced by a civil and criminal judiciary under a European Attorney-General. Seat of government would be Geneva; language of government would be French; and as executive, there would be a small police-force type army and a bureaucracy of proto-Eurocrats:

> The cosmopolitan service would become the most ambitious career in which young men of talent could engage; it would appeal to the

imagination far beyond diplomacy or the Indian Civil Service, and would speedily be embraced by those who were most gifted by nature and most favoured by fortune.

(Lorimer 1884: 258)

Peace and disarmament were prerequisites, but Lorimer's European legislature would decide what was national; it would create unity through great public works projects – 'architectural structures, both sacred and secular, of prodigious magnitude and grandeur' – and by gradually dissolving the old great powers, 'protect and give freer scope to ethnic peculiarities, whilst their anti-national action would add to its strength'.

In this, Lorimer saw an opportunity for renewing Scottish identity and curbing metropolitan concentration. He had fought for the autonomy of the Scottish universities, and his *Institutes of Law* (1872) were grounded in the idea of the natural sociability of man, derived from Sir William Hamilton and the deductive tradition of the Scottish Enlightenment (Davie 1961). He was no ethnic nationalist – regarding the Anglo-Indians as the successors of the Anglo-Saxons – but his advocacy of proportional representation and female suffrage were part of an envisaged structure of government whose 'civic humanist' criteria were expert-led rather than participatory. In this, he agreed with his friend the theologian Thomas Erskine of Linlathen – the centre of a Scoto-French intellectual circle which included Chalmers, Guizot, Cousin, Carlyle and Madame de Staël – that the need was for men to be well governed rather than self-governed (Hanna 1877: II, 37).

Folkloric research was a notable prop to the national geist. Von Savigny, the Roman lawyer and Prussian Justice-Minister, was patron of the brothers Grimm and their activities. Lorimer shared such interests, but through the more 'civic', Ruskinian concern of architecture. His pioneering restoration of his 'Franco-Scottish' castle at Kellie in Fife in the 1870s, abandoning Victorian ornament for the functional craftsmanship of the seventeenth century, influenced his son Sir Robert Lorimer to lead a revival of the Scottish vernacular style, a theme taken up in the architectural manifestos of Geddes, Rennie Mackintosh and Robert Hurd, which – unusually in Europe – united the causes of modern and vernacular architecture, social planning and small nationalism. In Scotland this led to the formation in 1936 of the Saltire Society, whose programme repeated the ambitions of the eighteenth-century enlightenment, and was deeply aware of European developments in these areas.

BRYCE, GLADSTONE AND DIFFUSED SOVEREIGNTY

James Lorimer mourned that:

> When rational men cross the frontiers of the separate states of which
> they are citizens, [must they] of necessity leave their wits behind
> them and in all their more important relations with each other, revert
> to the condition of savages or sink to that of fools?

(Lorimer 1884: 186)

Some states tended more than others to behave like this. The English
tradition of sovereign power, from Hobbes via Bentham to Dicey, found
little good in more diffuse, localised traditions. But Lorimer was not
alone. His friend James Bryce (1838–1922), Professor of Civil Law at
Oxford, author of *The American Commonwealth* (1889), Liberal MP
and minister, and Ambassador to the USA, 1908–13, was another
wandering Scot who made himself at home from Armenia to South
Africa. His concept of politics – derived from his studies in the history
of the Holy Roman Empire – was one in which sovereignty was divided
between the national, local or religious unit and the 'imperium'. Ideally,
this supreme, peace-keeping authority was shared between an elected
Emperor and a conciliar Church: the Ghibelline position found in the
empire–papacy conflicts of the fourteenth century. The German scholar
Thomas Kleinknecht has shown in his study *Imperiale und internationale Ordnung* (Kleinknecht 1985) that this ideal was common to
Bryce, Lord Acton and Gladstone, both through their classicism and
through their veneration for Dante, the Ghibelline poet, as the bridge
between the ancients and the moderns. Bryce applied his federalism to
the Holy Roman Empire, to America, to the abortive Imperial Federation
League and to home rule for Ireland – and ultimately to the League of
Nations ideal (Kleinknecht 1985: 103–7).

  Bryce's Glasgow education was, like Lorimer's, firmly in the
'common sense' tradition. His philosophy professor, Robert Buchanan,
carried on the ideas of Thomas Reid, and this influence, like Lorimer's
architectural interests, repeated the epic, folkloric preoccupations of the
Ossianic episode (Fisher 1927: I, 16). Scots lawyers, influenced by
Savigny, interested themselves – particularly in the 1870s and 1880s –
in antiquarianism and the recovery of the oral tradition, trying to
discover within the popular tradition an expression of a 'positive law'
(Lorimer 1872, 1880: 50). Bryce read *Ossian* and attempted to learn
Gaelic; his friend Aeneas Mackay (of a famous Scots-Dutch family),
later Professor of Constitutional Law at Edinburgh, helped found the
Scottish Historical Association and the Scottish Texts Society in the

1880s. John Veitch, Buchanan's successor at Glasgow and Hamilton's biographer, was also an authority on Border history and the ballad tradition.

This merging of the 'improving' and the mythic helps account for W.E. Gladstone's command of the 'Celtic fringe'; his combination of the civic and the epic resonated where community identity and the oral tradition were strong. Approval of his Irish home rule policy, despite militant Protestant traditions, set in motion the Catholic-radical alignment of Scottish politics, influential right up to the present day (Gallagher 1987: 70ff.). To his 'scientific' liberal contemporaries, Gladstone's Irish policy was intolerable, but his 'European sense', of which J.L. Hammond has written, was as consonant with Scots, Irish or Welsh ideas of identity as it was incompatible with 'Anglo-Saxonism' or business-led imperialism. It is difficult to pin ideology on the 'old parliamentary hand', but his sense of 'Christendom', of 'international public right' diffused among the European nations, and of self-government (initially among religious groups; latterly among nations) accords with the Scottish tradition (Harvie 1990a: 164–70).

GEDDES, KOHR, SCHUMACHER AND THE ECOLOGICAL REGION

Civic virtue was challenged by the rapid growth of industrial Britain, which provoked horror from observers. 'Here civilisation makes its miracles', noted Alexis de Tocqueville after a visit to Manchester in 1835, 'and civilised man is turned back almost into a savage.' The process subverted the eighteenth-century 'improver's notion of creating communities which were "harmoniously balanced" between industry and agriculture' (Tocqueville 1835, 1954: 108), yet 'balance' was demanded in the relation of the industrial region to its surrounding environment. Pollution was spread by the insatiable demand of industry for fuel and water, and its failure adequately – or at all – to reprocess its wastes. Textiles generated effluent; mineral extraction caused subsidence and created undrained swamps, which bred contagious diseases.

Manchester became symbolically important not only because it was the 'shock city' of first-stage industrialisation; it was where these problems were confronted by the ideology of a 'managed' society which the Scottish enlightenment was still producing. A figure such as the Edinburgh-educated Dr James Phillips Kay, later Sir James Kay-Shuttleworth, critic of health conditions in the cotton industry and Manchester, public health and later educational reformer, links the two. Such a 'civic consciousness' was less developed in industrial Europe.

Most industrial cities in Britain had clean water supplies by the 1870s and adequate sewage treatment plants. It took until the 1900s for the German Ruhr region to reach a similar stage, and its replanning only took place after 1919 (Rommelspacher 1993).

Even the infant British urban reform movement had a strong literary and transcendental dimension. Chalmers' *Christian and Civic Economy* (1821–6) preceded the polemics of Carlyle and the didactic fiction of the Christian Socialists, although Chalmers' contention that the problem of poverty could still be tackled on a parochial scale was falsified by the impact of cyclical depressions and mass unemployment. Carlyle's critique of *laissez-faire* got a second wind and an economic/ideological context in the 1850s and 1860s with the writing and lecturing of John Ruskin, from his *Unto This Last* (1861) onwards (Harrison 1905: 6). Like Hegelianism, this had a particularly strong impact on Oxford, where Ruskin was Slade Professor of Fine Art after 1867. Ruskin was a close friend of the great public health reformer Sir John Simon, and the first analysis of his economics was written in 1881 by another arch-systemiser, Patrick Geddes, in Scotland (Middlemass 1965: 30ff.).

Geddes started off as a follower of Auguste Comte, whose own political aims were highly centralised and elitist, but he was more deeply influenced by French regional geography, Carlyle's civic human-ist element and Ruskin's 'ecological economics'. A figure of quite remarkable range of reference and influence, Geddes not only bridged positivism, Fabian planning and Celtic literary nationalism, he revived the Scottish tradition of 'civic virtue' in the *polis*, and the intercon-nection of internal and external federalism (Meller 1973: 291–315). He borrowed his classification of human activity into place, work and folk from Le Play, but then extended this into his analysis of city types as palaeotechnic and neotechnic, something which was to be of enduring significance among town planners. Geddes's synoptic intellect was fortunate in attracting the sponsorship of wealthy patrons, including Andrew Carnegie, and his influence was significant, if diffuse, on the generation of town planners and geographers who came to maturity after the First World War: Patrick Abercrombie, H.J. Fleure, Raymond Unwin, Frank Mears and C.B. Fawcett, whose *The Provinces of England* (1921) was the first fully worked out scheme for English regional government (Meller 1990: 127–37).

Geddes's planning approach was eccentric to the 'nationalist' main-stream in being self-avowedly 'biocentric', something which came into its own in the 1970s with a critique of unplanned industrialisation and collectivist 'growth strategies' which were held to have shattered the internal consistency of socio- and eco-systems. Most notable was that of E.F. Schumacher, in *Small is Beautiful* (1973), but Schumacher was in turn the follower of Leopold Kohr, the Austrian economist, who had spent part of the 1930s assisting the Catalans in their vain struggle against Franco.

Around 1939 to 1940 the challenge of fascism and intellectual disillusion with communism produced a brief period of intense debate about pluralism and federalism. Various schemes of world government were advanced as a check to fascism, notably Clarence Streit's *Union Now* (1939), and R.W.G. MacKay's *Federal Union* (1940). The Left Book Club produced E.D. Simon's *The Smaller Democracies of Europe* (1939), explicitly modelled on James Bryce's *Modern Democracies* (1922). This concentrated on Switzerland, Denmark and Sweden, tracing civic consciousness from the village assembly to the national parliaments. It was the work of the leader of Manchester liberalism, later Lord Simon of Wythenshawe, and spelt out many of the decentralist themes which were to be raised by the Common Wealth movement, and the revival of Scottish nationalism, during the Second World War (Simon 1939: 176).

Such federalist schemes, backed within the Labour party by Robert Fraser, reflected the influence of the welfare states of the southern hemisphere on contemporary socialist politics – MacKay was also Australian, as was Michael Young, author of Labour's 1945 manifesto. Fraser and the Yorkshire anarchist Herbert Read became associated with Kohr, who argued, in his 1941 manifesto 'Disunion Now', published in a Catholic magazine in New York, for a cantonal Europe with governmental units of no more than 5 to 9 millions, in which ethnic divisions would be nullified through the creation of 'appropriate' units of government (Kohr 1941, 1991).

After the war Kohr came to Wales, where his ideas were taken up and strongly pressed by Plaid Cymru under the leadership of Gwynfor Evans. They emerged explicitly in 1957 in *The Breakdown of Nations*, in which he argued that the institutions of the large-scale nation-state explicitly frustrated both the ecological balance of society, and the civic development of the individual:

It is not poverty that is our problem. It is the *vast spread* of poverty. It is not unemployment but the *dimension* of modern unemployment which is the scandal; not hunger but the terrifying *number* afflicted by it; not depression but its world-encircling *magnitude*; not war but the atomic *scale* of war. In other words, the real problem of our time is not material but dimensional. It is one of scale, one of proportions, one of size; not a problem of any particular system, ideology or leadership. And since the size, the scale of social complexity takes its dimension from the society it afflicts, it follows that the only way of coping with it is, in analogy with the altitude disease, to bring the size of the afflicted society down to proportions within which man with his limited stature can once again assume control over it.

(Osmond and Graham 1984: 23f.)

In the 1960s and 1970s this interpretation influenced 'green' politics throughout Europe, an approach perhaps endorsed by the fact that Green parties have been far more successful at regional than at national level.

THE SMALLER NATIONS AFTER VERSAILLES

Some shifts towards such a regionalist or small-national ideology had been visible immediately before the First World War: in the virtual creation of Switzerland, the autonomy of Iceland, Norwegian and (partly) Finnish freedom. British 'home rule all round', and various attempts to sort out the Habsburg Empire counted as attempts to cope with the complexity of multinational and partly urban societies. Stanley Leathes concluded in his section of the *Cambridge Modern History* that,

Compared with these spontaneous manifestations of separatist feeling and national aspirations, the Pangermanic and Panslavonic movements seem pale and ineffective results of academic or interested propaganda.

(Leathes' Introduction in Ward 1910: 11)

But the models chosen for the post-war, succession states were essentially ethnic and centralised. Few federative states were created at Versailles – and attempts to do so in territories which must have seemed promising, such as Czechoslovakia and Jugoslavia, were foiled. Despite Slovak unease, the Czechoslovaks opted for a unitary state, with a Minister for Slovakia (along the lines of the Secretary for Scotland) and with a subordinate diet for the Ruthenian (Ukrainian) minority in the Bukovina. In Jugoslavia the Croats had proposed a loose federation of ethnic groups, but were (narrowly) outvoted in the Constitutional Convention by the Serbs and their allies, who imposed a centralised constitutional monarchy. The deciding factor was that the Czechs (thanks to Masaryk's secret diplomacy) and the Serbs had been on the side of the Allied 'winners', while the Croats had always been identified with the Austrian Empire. Constitutionalists also believed that the opinions of minorities could best be expressed by 'proper' representation in the legislature, both 'mechanically', in terms of the voting system, or by electoral arrangements which gave particular power to the intellectual elites. Hence the 'new democracies' were sustained, almost uniformly, by proportional representation systems of baffling complexity (Headlam-Morley 1928: 67, 97ff.).

There was little prospect of permanence. Too much of the Versailles settlement was grounded on who owed what, and to whom. Crude efforts in *Machtpolitik* soon moved in. Only one minority, the Finnish (but ethnically and linguistically Swedish) Åland Islanders, had rights granted them that were to be respected over time, as the result of a state treaty between Finland and Sweden (Modeen 1991: 153–68). More typical was the Italian policy in the former South Tyrol, following expulsion from their putative empire in Asia Minor. The unwary visitor (and none of the tourist brochures will tell him or her anything about it) will even today find in the highly-autonomous 'special region' a model fascist town in the suburbs of Bolzano: a glittering white triumphal arch, semi-modern movement law courts fronted by Victor Emmanuel on a prancing horse. It is, appropriately, inhabited by model fascists: Mussolini shifted the people of the Pontine marshes into the Tyrolese mountains, and his heirs, the Italian Social Movement, are the opposition party in the province (Ludwig 1992: 31–4).

Federalism was thin on the ground and (outside Switzerland) getting thinner. The Austrian rump-republic, which tried to stick with the principle, was overthrown in 1934 by the clerico-fascists under Dollfuss. In 1938 they succumbed to the real thing. Fascism made localist appeals but then eliminated such regional autonomy as existed (mainly in the educational sphere) with all the energy of liberal nationalism. Mussolini retained the centralised Italian state while the Nazis abolished the *Länder* within a month of taking power. Their attitudes to German regionalism were a mixture of British 'cultural regionalism' and French Jacobinism. Entertainment films and tourism encouraged by motorisation and *Autobahnen* stressed regional variety within Volkish limits; the Bavarian film studios still produced countless *Bauernkömodien* in which the Bürgermeister of Hicksdorf was shown up as a clown, when the real thing was a 150 per cent party member. In *Mein Kampf*, Hitler praised locality and tradition; but was careful to dwell even more on the 'German' identity that was derived from military service (Shand 1984: 193; Hitler 1925–7, 1939). What the railway had been to the liberal epoch, the road was to the Nazi New Order: 'Roads have always been the expression of a race's culture and living standards. Only the best roads have lasting value, and only such roads deserve to be seen as the historical and cultural creations of a great empire' (Shand 1984: 196).

Under this meta-European level, conquered countries were ruthlessly exploited and dispossessed with a view to future colonisation by re-peasantised Germans. This clashed with Arthur Rosenberg's plan to win the subject-nationalities of the Soviets to the German side and, since few Germans anyway wanted to be peasants, the result was stasis. The Nazi racist utopia was realised only in a negative sense, by mass inmigration from old settlements in south-eastern Europe.

In the West, potentially troublesome states were cowed into alliances, maintaining some degree of internal freedom. So Denmark and Finland preserved their democratic institutions, others obtained a semi-autonomy under quasi-fascist regimes, as in France, Croatia and Slovakia. The Nazis and their allies showed some sympathy for particularist movements which could be used to break up the greater nations – precisely the opposite of what Franco's Falangists were doing in Spain. The Pétain government tried to substitute 'work, family, region and fatherland' for 'liberty, equality and fraternity', and looked with some favour on Breton nationalism. This did not help the regional ideal when liberation came (Fitzmaurice 1981; Dickinson 1967: 230; Mowat 1966: 199–210).

THE SUPERPOWER UTOPIAS

The aftermath of the Second World War was dominated not by world unity, nor by multiple Switzerlands, but by two highly ideological superpowers. Their internal politics are beyond the scope of this book, but their influence is not, since in Britain the decentralist enthusiasms of such groups as Common Wealth were sapped by the support won by the 'planning' of the Soviet Union, and the boost that this gave to socialist ideas (Calder 1969, 1971: 401–5). Had the cross-class identity of regionalism any role in the communist order which would dominate Eastern Europe for over forty years, with the aim of producing a 'new socialist man'? Could it survive the imposition of the 'Americanism' which turned an German immigrant of the 1920s into a loyal GI scrambling from a landing-craft in Normandy?

The answer to the first was emphatically no. Local government was overall viewed as a reflex of party and industrial requirements, and imposed without regard to 'community'. The last vestiges of federal East Germany, for example, were abolished in 1952. Where nominal concessions were made, as in Stalin's constitution of 1936, these applied to the twenty or so significant *ethnies* within the Soviet Union, out of 140 nationalities. The product of Tsarist conquest in the nineteenth century and the Nazi-Soviet pact, these all had distinctive linguistic, ethnic and religious roots, roles in past Russian history, and differing experiences of the Soviet system. These – as a fictional sovereignty which suddenly became real – would become part of their reckoning with the post-1986 period of *perestroika* and *glasnost* (Brzezinski 1989).

The 'non-dominant' races could roughly be divided into six main groups: the Baltic republics, the south-western borderlands (Ukraine, Belorussia, Moldavia), Transcaucasia, Muslim Central Asia, Non-Russians of the Russian Republic, and the 'Diaspora Nationalities' – the Jews and Crimean Tartars (Smith 1991). How did their national movements develop across the land mass of the former Soviet Union, and to what extent did they correspond to the experience of cognate groups in Western Europe? One thing is immediately apparent. The minorities most urbanised and closest geographically and politically to the West – notably the now-independent Baltic republics – almost uniformly underwent a 'post-industrial' decline in population growth, while those Central Asian republics strongly Islamic in character, and effectively only urbanised since the Second World War, saw dramatic population increases. The Estonians, the wealthiest group in the old USSR, grew by barely 4 per cent between 1959 and 1989, from just under to just over one million. The Uzbeks, statistically the poorest, increased from six to nearly seventeen millions, despite truly horrendous economic and ecological conditions. In other words, the Soviet Union was less the 'Second World' than something that ran the gamut between the lower end of the 'developed world' and the depths of 'Third World' underdevelopment. This happened despite centralised economic policies, the forcible movement of peoples, the systematic destruction, particularly under Stalin, of regional and ethnic elites, and the 'Russification' (or at any rate rendering into Cyrillic script) of subordinate languages.

What were, in the 1980s, the motives behind 'national' challenges to these centralising pressures? Poets, historians and clergy – the intellectual elite of *pre-industrial*, not just *pre-communist* Russia – predominated in the 'reform' movements, with a few ecological and civil rights activists thrown in; economists and technocrats were conspicuous by their absence, although a bit more salient in the Baltics. Why was this? There was some sort of parallel with the 'poet and priest' nationalist intelligentsia in Ireland under British rule – although the British also left behind an efficient and honest civil service. Ireland also provides a prototype of 'plantation' – something widely practised for economic reasons in the nineteenth-century British Empire. As well as Mussolini's activities in the Tyrol, Franco tried to do something similar in Spain after 1939, encouraging a Castilian migration into Cataluña which made up about 40 per cent of its population by 1980 (Stewart 1977, 1989; Gallagher 1991: 121f.).

But Falangism was relatively porous. In the British colonies, native administrative elites developed through the occupier's social overhead capital: the infrastructure, distribution and educational systems. In Russia not only was everything on a much vaster scale, but the interlocking specialisms of the Soviet command-and-barter economy both overemphasised capital-goods industry, and made such incremental innovations difficult. Exploring the pre-1986 economic and social situation requires a two-track approach, both regional and dealing with such institutions as the army, the economic bureaucracy, the KGB and the Communist party itself.

Soviet society *was* capable of major technological advance – witness their space programme or urban transportation. The Soviet Union's external debt, even in 1991, was *per capita* much lower than that of most nations; most of the collapse in the supply of consumer goods occurred *after perestroika*. Yet there was no reformist cadre to bring the Soviets gently around to the application of gradualist reform. Almost the opposite. Such decentralist initiatives as had developed under the 'semi-mixed' New Economic Policy of the 1920s ended with the combination of centralised planning and political terror in the 1930s (Acton 1992: 162–70).

Russia was never a reformist society; the rudiments of a *polis* in the *zemstvo* (county council) system created in 1864 were never strong enough to deflect central determination. Education was removed from their control in 1869 and, as in parts of Germany, restrictive voting systems were introduced. Particularism, however, paralysed most efforts at centralised reform (Freeze 1992). Coercion was one answer to this, and Stalin's butchery had its pre- or non-revolutionary precedents, like the Turkish massacre of 1.5 million Armenians in 1915; and also harnessed other inter-ethnic feuds. Brezhnev anaesthetised such problems through corruption and 'benign neglect' until the environmental costs of Soviet giantism – whether Chernobyl, or the disappearance of most of the Aral Sea, or oil-shale mining in Estonia – leaped on to the backs of his successors.

But although ecology as well as national issues brought people on to the streets, demonstrations couldn't be counted on to produce qualified economists. Even fierce critics of the old order like the *Financial Times*'s John Lloyd were writing by 1991 that the fraying strands of the command economy were all that held the Russian federation together. The beneficiaries of 'instant market economics' were black marketeers and outright criminals, not a few of whom transformed their regional mafias into nationalist movements. 'Civic virtue' was notable only for its absence (Brzezinski 1989).

The right of individual states to secede, which in 1990–1 broke up the Soviet Union, had plunged America into a near-total war in 1861–5: an ominous precedent. Granted a diametrically opposed economic system, certain other 'integrationist' themes are common to Russia and the United States. Communists of Lenin's generation were quick to identify with the expansion both of the federal power and of supra-regional industrial concerns such as Ford and the oil and power companies. The Russians' attempt to impose their language and thereby to create the New Soviet Man was a more timid version of the American 'melting-pot' indoctrination which operated very successfully for the first two-thirds of this century. Lenin's enthusiasm for F.W. Taylor's 'scientific management' was explicitly a rejection of any sort of group identity outwith the industrial structure. But the dysfunctions of a centralised and militarised economy, and the continuing failure of collectivised agriculture to meet its targets, meant that the Soviet economy had become dependent on agricultural imports from America by the mid-1960s (Mowat 1966: 317–20).

In America, federalism had been understood, ever since Hamilton and Madison's *Federalist Papers* as a centralising impulse, yet a US-type federal structure was adopted by West Germany in 1949, explicitly to weaken the centralism which was thought to stand behind national aggressiveness. In fact, all of the larger 'white dominions' – Canada (1867), Australia (1908) and South Africa (1908) – had developed 'American' types of federalism. But the USA's adoption of New Deal interventionism further enhanced the federal government at the expense of the states. In part, this was because social reform had its roots in the 'civic' or 'progressive' movement which had also inspired urban reformers such as Geddes, but which could not be accommodated in the existing structure of states. American 'regionalism' tended to be, in contrast, a conservative, anti-urban movement – much associated with the revival of southern culture after 1918.

The federal impulse reached a climax in the Kennedy–Johnson years, Johnson's 'Great Society' programme of 1964 being also, intriguingly, a misreading of Graham Wallas's book of that name (1914), in which he had construed 'great' as 'mass' and warned against bureaucracy and centralisation. In the 1960s, however, a countervailing power also got under way with 'regional' economic development in areas such as Texas and California, influenced by oil extraction and computer-based high technology, along with a revulsion against 'big government' and

Washington rule. The 'civic' critique of the constitution was sapped by the centrifugal 'suburbanisation' of the city population. Moreover, the new immigrants – chiefly Hispanics – have proved less and less assimilable within the structures of American patriotism, and the prospect has now arisen of linguistically distinctive regions on the European pattern. The negotiation of a customs union with Canada in 1991, on the pattern of the Treaty of Rome, highlighted other forces making for disunity, with the oil-based renaissance of Alberta and the reassertion of *Québecois* nationalism in the 1960s. The *Parti Québecois*, dismissed in the 1960s as parochial conservatives, swept forward to form a government under René Lévesque in 1978. Its combination of cultural politics and pragmatic, state-led, high-technology industrialisation showed closer – and conscious – parallels to European regionalism than to the North American tradition. Whether Quebec can be contained within the Canadian structure is deeply uncertain.

Is it ominous that civic ideologies aiming at the reform of 'subordinate' government seem to appear on the scene just before huge upheavals – whose causes lie in the same context – shatter the whole political community? Rousseau on Corsica precedes the French Revolution; de Tocqueville's decentralisation is followed by large-scale wars of national unity; the 'civic movement' of the 1900s by the First World War; the debate on federal union by the Second World War. The campaign for civic identity in Eastern Europe in 1989–91 ended in a headlong plunge into market economics – characterised by one Russian commentator as 'learning to swim by diving overboard in a storm' – and quickly released the unlovely genie of ethnic politics. In turn, will the inevitable frustrations of the market utopia and nationalism bring new civic and co-operative movements – on the lines of the EC – into being? Civic movements are the terrain of Machiavelli's foxes; wars and revolutions of his lions. What have the West European foxes created during the 'nuclear peace' since 1945 that the emergent democracies, and the residual idealists of the euphemistically titled 'developing world', can copy?

5 Regionalism and European unity

POST-HISTORICAL EUROPE

By 1992 one spectre had given up haunting Europe. It was promptly replaced by several more, alarmingly unpredictable: nationalism, refugees, terrorism, ecological horrors of one sort or another. Even granted the negotiation of these problems, Professor J.G.A. Pocock, the New Zealand-born historian of *The Machiavellian Moment*, talked in a moving and pessimistic essay of 'the tunnel at the end of the light', of a 'post-historical' Europe in which the affluent

> wander as tourists – which is to say consumers of images – from one historical culture to another, delightfully free from the need to commit themselves to any. Meanwhile the non-affluent form under-classes, pools of labour ebbing from one area of underemployment to another . . . capable at best of the specialist activisms which constitute populism but not democracy.
>
> (Pocock 1991: 10)

Against these, could there be invoked one benign spectre, of Pocockian pedigree, which could be called 'bourgeois regionalism'? The term itself was ambiguous. 'Bourgeois' *qua* dynamic individualism or *qua* civic humanism? But the phenomenon was new, distinct both from the 'utopianism' of command-economy socialism (which might recognise ethnic groups, but rarely recognised regional political identity) and the marketised dystopia which Pocock feared. Did it have a problem-solving potential beyond that of 'narrow' nationalism?

In the 1970s, the European Community's 'regional' element was a mission to Pocock's 'non-affluent', intended to keep them harmless and, if possible, at home. Even when seen positively, the 'regional issue' tended to formulate itself as the 'historic' regions – Scotland, Brittany, Corsica, etc. – versus their respective central states. These were the regions which Michael Hechter (borrowing from the geographers' 'core-periphery' paradigms) christened 'internal colonies', over-rich in 'problem areas', whether small peasant farms – Ireland, Southern Italy, Brittany – or old industrial concerns – the Borinage, the Ruhr, Limburg (Hechter 1975: 33; Blaschke 1980; Elkar 1981; Gerdes 1980). Through the pressure of French politicians, the former Gaullist Premier Edgar Faure in particular, these were in 1978 given a role when the Council of Europe set up the Standing Conference of Local and Regional Authorities of Europe (CLRAE). The regions, Faure wrote upliftingly, 'are in a good position to woo public opinion back to the European cause; what this lacks is popular affection, the capacity to be felt by the heart, to adapt Pascal's remark about God' (Council of Europe 1986: 4).

The regions which came to prominence in the 1980s, however, were something quite different, natural 'basins' of economic and social activity which seemed more 'bourgeois' than nation-states deformed by the residues of aristocracy, army and empire. Hechter's 1981 equivalent was surely Martin Wiener, whose *English Culture and the Decline of the Industrial Spirit*, arguing precisely thus, attained a totemic quality, not only among the court of Mrs Thatcher (Wiener 1981; Sillars 1985: 123; Dahrendorf 1984: 18ff.).

After 1985, under a 'second wind' following the integration of its new Mediterranean members, the Community's drive to the federal organisation of economic and fiscal policy accelerated. Implicitly, this trenched on the powers of existing nation-states, but neither Germany nor France quarrelled with it: the Germans because they didn't want to advertise the 'national' element in their drive to unity; the French because they were already in process of domestic decentralisation. The British Conservative government remained opposed both to European and internal federalism, but its economic record scarcely made it an argument for centralism.

The Maastricht Treaty in December 1991 held by the principle of subsidiarity, and underlined what it meant by that by proposing an advisory Council of the European Regions, on a par with the European Social and Economic Council. This package was rejected by Denmark in May 1992, in part for 'British' reasons, in part because it was not considered federal enough. The 'subsidiarity' element – in a vague and unspecified form – was subsequently strengthened early in October 1992. This was claimed as a success by the British government, but the other European powers, particularly Germany, increasingly dominated by the Social Democrat-controlled Bundesrat, continued to regard Maastricht as devolving decision-making to a regional level. Who would sit on the proposed Council of the Regions? Europe insisted on regional elected representatives; the British government tried to secure centrally nominated ministers and civil servants, and proposed a bias in favour of the Scots and the Welsh in an attempt to buy off demands for local parliaments. Meanwhile the sweeping gains of the regional 'Leagues' in Italy placed the whole future of that state in jeopardy (*Maastricht Treaty* 1992: Article 198a; Gallagher 1992).

To this were added two national problematics. Germany, the pioneer of federalism within Europe, had been roughly equal in population to Italy, France and Great Britain. After 1990 it became, at 80 million, the apologetic Leviathan of the Community. One way of coping with this imbalance was to take the weak patriotism of the Germans at face value, and encourage regionalisation within the Community. But was German regionalism really a match for the country's much-feared nationalism, as unification ran into trouble, the internal and external financial demands on the *Bund* increased, and as an influx of refugees from Romania and Jugoslavia revived the extreme right (Stares 1992: 33ff.)?

In Britain, successive Conservative governments found no reason to apologise for a highly centralised state, although a sense of separate identity took Scotland, Wales and Northern Ireland to a point at which secession seemed more plausible than any continuation of the status quo. Instead of pursuing some form of regionalism or federalism within England, which could enable integration with European practice, Conservative policy implied a reversal to administrative Jacobinism. Under the 'banner headline' of privatisation, this in fact implied the 'nationalisation' of whole tranches of local government activity (health provision and education) with only weak powers being left at a local level of unco-ordinated, single-function bodies (Crouch and Marquand 1989: vii–xi).

THE 'NEW' REGIONS

The definition of 'region' in 1980 was still a summation of public-sphere attempts to preserve cultural values and to combat 'uneven development'. Of the regions in typical symposia of the period, only about 10 per cent, going by population, were 'advanced' in terms of the standards of the 'predominant power' to which they were attached. Cataluña and Südtirol certainly were, but that wasn't why they were there. Yet by 1980 effective devolution in Italy was scarcely a decade old; the Spanish constitution with its provincial government provisions had only just been passed, in 1978. Mitterrand had still to come to power in France on a programme of decentralisation, but French civil servants and *ENArques* (graduates of the Ecole Nationale d'Administration) were active studying administrative devolution, nationalist and federal movements elsewhere in Europe, including (embarrassingly) Scotland (Leruez 1983).

There is a time-lag in any far-reaching institutional innovation. Sir Robert Calderwood, its Chief Executive, said that it took from 1974 to 1984 to 'run in' the administrative machinery of Strathclyde Region. This phase lasted up to 1980 and had to precede the promotion of functioning federal or semi-federal structures in the major European states. Certain historical themes reasserted themselves, as alternatives to individualist capitalism and nationalism, and interest in the 'civic humanism' studied by Pocock and his colleagues grew as the command economies decayed. The Machiavellian ideal of 'civic virtue' was revived, although the necessary qualities of government were, ironically, best exemplified in the 'civic humanism' of the towns – Bologna, Perugia, Siena – of the Italian 'red belt' (King 1987: 177, 199; Haycraft 1987: 19ff.).

The impact of the post-war 'European movement' seemed to confirm Leopold Kohr's notion of the constitutive nature of political institutions. There were three main rationalisations of governmental style. The French pattern, exemplified by Jean Monnet, was of a highly trained 'prefectorial' elite moving from the *hautes écoles* to the *départements* and then, via the national level of the Commissariat du Plan, to Brussels. The 'Anglo-American' pattern of autonomous administration on the other hand was imposed on post-Second World War Germany in the more structured form of federalism. This was initially unpopular among the German electorate – nationalist and *gesamtdeutsch* (union-favouring) Social Democrat alike – with the result that the French model remained unchallenged in the 1960s, when it appeared to secure an unparalleled rate of industrialisation (Sampson 1968: 329ff.; Marsh 1989: 79). Thirdly, and least obtrusively, there was the initiative of the small states, with the Benelux and Nordic customs and passport unions being accomplished in 1945 and 1962 respectively. The most 'European' ministers of the 1950s and 1960s – Spaak, de Gasperi, Strauss – were strongly regional in background (Sampson 1968: 21–7, 48). Adenauer, the Rhineland Catholic, had little time for the 'Prussians', red or otherwise; despite his identification with French nationalism, even de Gaulle had certain Breton loyalties (Milward 1992: 318–44; Mayo 1974: 20ff.).

That the issue of regional government led to the final toppling of de Gaulle in 1969 was no coincidence. The year 1968 had been, overall, a disaster for the millennial left: the French electorate crushed the students and confirmed Gaullism; the suppression of the Prague Spring showed how unreformable Soviet communism was. The pragmatic mix of Europeanism and the nation-state claimed by Milward as the basis of the EEC seemed validated – for the time being. In the following decade, the slackening of state-sponsored industrialisation; the shift towards the multinational company; the international management of finance and information; the emergence of new social and ecological imperatives, and of a European identity: all these weakened the nation-state. De Rougemont's definition of the region as 'the space for civic participation' reflected the potential expansion and mobilisation of the bourgeoisie so that it became a *citizenry* (rather than the layered structure of a wealthy economic elite dominating a fluctuating underclass of the metropolis). This offered another approach to liberating and empowering the contiguous areas of, say, students and trainees, women, immigrants; it adumbrated duties and rights which are universal as well as specific (de Rougemont 1977, 1983: 219).

There remained, however, a tension at the heart of the 'bourgeois region', between the civic and the economic. The emergent regions *actually* were predominantly urban; concerned with manufacture, financial services and trade, at the innovative edge of the capital goods industries. For purposes of research and training, marketing and maintaining social acceptability, the 'cultures' of modern multinational firms were also moving in a 'civic' direction, but incompatibilities remained. When 'cultured' multinational met 'bourgeois' region, whose values won out (Business International 1986: 154)?

SPANISH AND FRENCH SEMI-FEDERALISM

In 1957, at the time of the Treaty of Rome, Spain was a fossil of inter-war fascism. During and after the Civil War, Franco had crushed the Basque and Catalan autonomists with extreme brutality, and had attempted, by 'plantation' and linguistic suppression, to diminish their identity. This only served to provoke a determined armed-force reaction from the Basques from the 1960s on, which in 1973 claimed the life of Admiral Carrero Blanco, Franco's designated successor, a setback from which the ailing dictator and his regime never recovered (Gallagher 1991: 119–33).

After Franco's death, in 1978, Adolfo Suarez, heading a centre-right Christian Democrat government, with the backing of the young king, created democratic institutions throughout Spain and offered to devolve limited powers to its seventeen 'communities'. He found that the politics of the two 'historic nationalities' were so entrenched that he was forced to offer them the charters which set up the 'Autonomous Communities' in Cataluña and, after a fiercer conflict, in Euskadi (1980). This was not only a direct assault on the centralisation of the Franco regime: it also conflicted with the centralised tradition of the Spanish socialists (PSOE) who took over in 1981; and it failed to halt the continuing conflict in Euskadi. Spain, in fact, shows the gamut of styles of regions, from the 'European Spain' of Cataluña, with its 'bourgeois regionalist' regime of Jordi Pujol, to the backwardness of Galicia, which has a dialect akin to Portuguese, and compares itself with Ireland or the Scottish highlands. Galicia's conservative identity has been used as the basis of a right-wing revival by the former Francoist minister Manuel Fraga. On the other hand, the PSOE has also stressed its own affinity with Andalusia. The 'big spending' of Olympic Year, 1992, was in a sense an inter-regional competition, with Cataluña – 'a country in Spain' – promoting the Olympics, and the PSOE government boosting Andalusia through Expo '92 and the new TGV link from Madrid. Ironically, in the country most associated with it, the anarchist tradition had, save in Euskadi, almost died out (Gallagher 1991: 132).

Despite the sophistication of regional studies in France, among geographers and the *Annales* school of historians, the system of local government remained that of 1792, the country being divided into ninety-six *départements*, each under a Paris-appointed *préfet*. In contrast to Germany, where 80 per cent of taxation was raised locally, only 15 per cent was so raised. For planning purposes, the *départements* were amalgamated into 22 regions in 1964, each under a superior grade of *préfet*, and in 1971–2, under Georges Pompidou, these were granted indirectly elected advisory regional councils. At every stage, however, these arrangements reflected the convenience of the central state, the *préfet* being as much a manager of local politics as an administrator, and the boundaries of the regions being specifically drawn to avoid any resemblance to the old cultural provinces. By 1968 this had led to sporadic outbreaks of armed resistance in Brittany and Corsica, and to a general shift on the left towards decentralisation. In 1982 wide powers, greater than those enjoyed by the 'special' regions in Italy (which were prevented from opening links with Brussels), were granted to elected regional councils, one of the first acts of the Mitterrand government, at that time headed by a notable regional leader, Pierre Mauroy, former Mayor of Lille (Ardagh 1982, 1986: 187–205; Raffarin 1988; Colletis 1993).

Even in 1992 it was difficult to see precisely where this would lead. Despite their limited staffs, the bigger regions, such as Rhône-Alpes, had made notable progress in areas such as transport, research and education; others, such as Upper and Lower Normandy, with a quarter of the Rhône-Alpes population, had scarcely begun to act. As in Spain, there were signs that a successful regionalisation would hit national identity. In the referendum on the Maastricht Treaty on 22 July 1992, regions such as Rhône-Alpes, Brittany and Alsace-Lorraine voted 'yes', while old industrial areas and traditional rural France remained hostile. On the other hand, the example of former Jugoslavia, and the memory of the Civil War, checked secessionist tendencies in Cataluña (Ludwig 1992).

BOURGEOIS REGIONALISM: GERMAN STYLE

The devolution of economic planning authority to regional legislatures seemed to validate the 'German model' which had gained complete acceptance by the 1970s. In 1987 German electors valued, above all else, their *Grundgesetz* or federal constitution; for the English (but not the Scots) the equivalent was the monarchy. The success of 'co-operative federalism' was partly due to the emergence of regional political elites as negotiators between various economic, political and environmental interest groups, and partly because the Bundesrepublik had developed a sophisticated system of federal oversight of Brussels legislation, through *Land* observers, Bundesrat discussion of EC affairs (amounting to 40 per cent of its business) and direct *Land* representation in Brussels bureaus (Bulmer 1986: 255–62).

Two such – the Saarland and Baden-Württemberg – were, in their 'European' policies, exemplary. With the Saarland, a series of relationships was built up on a geographical basis of shared interests by the German *Land* (run by the Social Democrats under the charismatic figure of Oskar Lafontaine since 1986), the French Region of Lorraine, created by the Mitterand reforms in 1982, and the Grand Duchy of Luxembourg. In the 'Four Motors', Baden-Württemberg created an intra-European confederation of regions specialising in high-technology – Baden-Württemberg, Lombardy, Rhône-Alpes, and Cataluña – to which Wales affiliated in March 1990.

The three regions in the Moselle valley represented the drastic industrial and environmental reorientation of post-Second World War politics in Europe. The river, only seasonally navigable by large craft, was until 1945 a critical international frontier and communications channel, heavily fortified, in the wars of 1870–1, 1914–18 and 1939–45. Following its occupation by the French, the Saarland voted overwhelmingly in 1935 for reunion with Nazi Germany, to the chagrin of such left-wing activists as remained (including the communist Erich Honecker), and a right-wing tradition remained dominant after its reunion with the Bundesrepublik was decided on by a 67 per cent to 33 per cent majority in October 1955.

After the creation of the European Coal and Steel Community in 1948, the Moselle was made navigable for 1,000-tonne barges and became an object of common interest and concern: as an industrial artery, a structuring factor in a near-continuous urban agglomeration, and an ecological problem. Similar political evolutions in the three states (socialism in the old mining areas surviving as an ethos of regional reconstruction), and shared aspects of cultural identity (German widespread as a second language, where not the first) have led to close co-operation, for example in local transport, common courses at universities, and pollution control (Hahn 1988; Lafontaine 1989).

In this a leading role was taken by Lafontaine. Physicist, nuclear disarmer, product of 1968, socialist rather than Social Democrat, the young Mayor of Saarbrücken who took over the leadership of the SPD in the early 1980s effectively cut out the Greens by adopting most of their programme. Similar collaborative movements are also under way, for example, between the German *Land* of Saxony and the Czech republic, centred on the Elbe, in the *Länderdreieck*; between Freiburg, Basel and Mulhouse, involving collaboration between Baden-Württemberg, Alsace and Canton Basel; and ArGe Alp (*Arbeitsgemeinschaft Alp Adria* – Taskforce Alp) involving (among others) Salzburg, Südtirol, the Veneto and Slovenia, and dealing with the area between the Alps and the Adriatic. Increasing pollution threats to rivers, the Alps and the Baltic Sea will promote further co-operation, which may in time create an intermediate level of authority, between region and European centre, more relevant than the old nation-state.

It did not, however, promote Lafontaine's own candidacy, against Helmut Kohl in the first all-German elections in December 1990, where Lafontaine's (perceptive) distrust of Kohl's optimism about the financial burden of German unity cost him the support of the East German working class, and meant the worst post-war result on record for the SPD.

THE FOUR MOTORS

By contrast, the Four Motors scheme reflected a non-geographical nexus of factors which became critically important within the European Community as it evolved towards a situation of 'mature' industrialisation. These were dominated by the functional requirements of multinational, or perhaps more correctly 'post-national', high-technology companies (Kodak, IBM, Daimler-Benz, etc.) which, along with the internationalisation of capital markets, rendered 'national' economic policies increasingly ineffective (Cooke and Morgan 1990; Esser 1989: 99; Sturm 1990: 5–9). 'Post-industrial culture' meant (either within the nation or the firm) the ability to select and 'steer' industrial development. This placed authority with a largely inter-changeable elite, dealing with areas of education, research and training, social and transportation infrastructure, and ecological balance. These came to have greater importance than traditional industrial and agri-cultural policy, and involved matters which had to be tackled at either European or regional level.

Baden-Württemberg's prominent role stemmed from its economic evolution. The local myth stresses the *absence* of natural resources – coal, iron, etc. – and a landscape of tiny agricultural units, the densest rural settlement in Europe. This deficit had to be made up through ingenuity, governmental policy and local political culture: the Swabian capacity for innovation or '*tüfteln*' and 'work and save', backed by government funds and organisation, promoting first locomotives and then the electricity, car and aviation industries (Bosch spark plugs and magnetos, the Benz automobile, the Zeppelin airship). The banking system channelled savings through a network of Kreissparkassen, Volksbanken, Genossenschaftsbanken. At the top of which pyramid is the Deutsche Bundesbank; although separated from federal government control, this is directed by a board consisting of eleven *Land* repre-sentatives out of twenty (Kloss 1976, 1982: 93).

The post-war economic situation encouraged industrial innovation. In contrast to Britain, the period after 1945 was one of skilled *immigration*: about 2 million refugees, first from Silesia, then from East Germany. Although bombing had been very severe, with the centres of most of the main cities devastated, this part of Germany, from Hesse south to Stuttgart, was in the American occupation zone, and greenfield sites were available to American industrial plants and the sort of American-style industries that, in their competitive, uncartelised nature, were quite new in German manufacturing (Berghahn 1988). Farms were rapidly converted first to part-time holdings, then to dwellings for industrial workers (Land Baden-Württemberg 1991). Even today the sheer range of industries is remarkable: a university town like Tübingen, for instance, with a population of 70,000, has besides the university and its clinics, factories producing washing-machines, machine-tools, musical instruments, and towelling in addition to several printing works, a railway- and two bus-maintenance depots.

This manufacturing variety (42 per cent of Baden-Württemberg's GNP is in manufacture, against about 24 per cent in the UK) was one favourable element: the social inequality encountered through the overdevelopment of a low-productivity, low value-added and low-paid service sector was avoided. Another, perhaps less welcome, factor was that industrialisation depended on the motor-car. Of Baden-Württemberg technical trade apprentices, over half go into the automobile field. Cars weren't just manufactured. They were the means whereby agricultural villages became dormitories for factories like Daimler-Benz's giant Sindelfingen plant – lessening the cost of workers' housing, and other demands on infrastructure. *Die Zeit* (15 June 1990) showed that 71 per cent of to-work journeys in Germany were made by car; that proportion would almost certainly be higher in 'industrial' Baden-Württemberg – virtually the 'Greater Stuttgart' city-region, from Heilbronn in the north to Tübingen in the south, from Karlsruhe in the west to Schwäbisch Gmünd in the east: one of the transportation/ land-use model regions so fashionable in the 1960s (Ellger 1983).

'Greater Stuttgart' fitted securely within the boundaries of the *Land* (as did its rival, the *Ruhrgebiet* within North Rhine-Westphalia). But *Länder* boundaries could inhibit co-operation. To the north there was a potentially far more dynamic region, at the confluence of the rivers Rhine, Main and Neckar, bounded by Wiesbaden, Mainz, Mannheim, Aschaffenburg and Frankfurt (with Europe's biggest airport), but authority was there divided between no less than four *Länder* (Rhineland-Palatinate, Hesse, Bavaria and Baden-Württemberg). There exists within the German *Grundgesetz* ('fundamental law') of 1949 a provision for the *Neugliederung der Bundesländer* (readjustment of *Land* frontiers), theoretically to cope with such problems, but only in the case of the creation of Baden-Württemberg in 1949–52 was this ever activated. In 1974 the Social-Liberal coalition brought in regional planning legislation which attempted to promote inter-*Länder* co-operation, but the return of the centre-right in 1982 made this a dead letter (Sturm 1988).

The concept of the 'Europe of the Regions' was sold by the Four Motors with all the energy one might expect of such well-heeled areas. A travelling exhibition commissioned by Baden-Württemberg in 1990 cost an estimated DM14 million. But what did the co-operation amount to? The agreement with the Welsh Office – not a full 'Motor' because it lacked a legislature – which was signed in Cardiff on 26 March 1990 contained clauses on economic co-operation and technical transfer, sharing of environmental information and research results, student and cultural exchanges (*Stuttgarter Zeitung*, 28 March 1990). Obviously in prospect was the sort of benefit which Rhône-Alpes had enjoyed, with a fibre-optic cable link which plugged it into Baden-Württemberg's sophisticated technology-transfer system, and the high level of techno-logical training which the establishment of the Stuttgart firm of Bosch's plant at Miskin near Cardiff seemed to promise (Harvie 1990b).

OUT OF STEP . . .

With the impact of the Single European Act and the imminence of some degree of European federalism, such developments were being seen as the norm within the European Community, and as a potential bridge both between the individual and the 'super-state', and between West and East Europe, through regional partnerships such as that between Baden-Württemberg and the restored *Land* of Saxony, and Saxony and the Czech Republic.

In this process, the United Kingdom was completely anomalous. In the 1940s the autonomy and resources of local authorities were drastically diminished through nationalisation and the welfare state. However, a general commitment to 'welfare citizenship' secured a devolution of socio-economic decision-making to professional groups (as with the universities, the lawyers and the doctors). This happened under the overall assumption of a 'British homogeneity' of political behaviour, although nationalist momentum meant that the Scottish Office continually accumulated powers, while a Welsh Office, under a cabinet minister, was added by Labour in 1964. In the 1960s two royal commissions suggested a pattern of regional councils, but only in Scotland was this carried out in 1974, without much enthusiasm on the part of the Scots, who really wanted home rule. For the first time, powers to assist economic development were granted, and supplemented in Scotland and Wales by Development Agencies. In 1979, however, a more ambitious project, to grant a measure of legislative devolution to Scotland and Wales, was rejected by the Welsh and carried by the Scots with an insufficiently large margin to pass it into law (although by a margin bigger than the Danish rejection, or the French endorsement, of Maastricht). This also, intriguingly, pointed out the considerable differences *within* Scotland, with Shetland and the Borders, both areas of strong local identity, voting 'no'. The outbreak of terrorism in Northern Ireland brought an end in 1972 to the autonomy that the province had enjoyed since 1922 (Harvie 1988: 49–55).

Under Mrs Thatcher, the role of the local state was drastic curtailed. The 'metropolitan counties' created by the 1974 Act abolished in 1986, including the Greater London Council, whic metropolis bereft of any unit for co-ordination and strategic planning. The effects of this were evident by 1990 in the catastrophic over-investment in office property and the deterioration of the public-transport system, which had in the 1930s been the prototype for cities in the rest of the world (Page 1991). The official rationale for this process was that 'market forces' (which acquired a totemic quality in the 1980s) would 'liberate' the individual from an allegedly bureaucratic state. In the event, bureaucracy increased in a haphazard way, with powers being accumulated by quangos, civil servants and 'watchdogs' over-looking the privatised utilities: a situation increasingly resembling that of English local government before rationalisation started in the 1880s. In Scotland and Wales the devolved administrations continued to accumulate powers – over the environment and higher education – which made them comparable to German *Länder*. They also established representations in Brussels, but without any elected authority: some-thing which seemed programmed to cause conflict when the European Communities, post-Maastricht, decided on what 'subsidiarity' would be based (Thomas 1991: 57–67).

6 A critical perspective

SOME REGIONS ARE MORE EQUAL THAN OTHERS

'Europe of the Regions'; 'Four Motors'; 'ArGe Alp': was there not an element of wishful thinking in these beguiling concepts? Was the dominance of 'core regions' less a pattern for future development than a 'one-off'? With very little to do with the small-scale, self-regulating political and ecological systems of Kohr and Schumacher? The 'bourgeois' regions – grouped around Switzerland – concentrated in themselves a disproportionately large amount of the investment and the organisational structures of a European multinational capitalism which now mattered more as an economic performer than all but the largest nation-states. In their science-fiction satire *The Space Merchants* (1953), Frederic Pohl and Cyril Kornbluth imagined a market dystopia in which great industrial concerns took over the roles of nation-states – General Motors was America, IG Farben was Germany – and advertising agencies acted as their diplomats and armies (Pohl and Kornbluth 1953, 1981). Were the 'Four Motors' not, in some respects, a prototype of this?

Baden-Württemberg, for example, prided itself on its small and medium-sized enterprises (SMEs), which bodies like the Steinbeis Foundation existed to aid, but this was different from the 'microcapitalism' of Emilia-Romagna and Tuscany. The health of the SMEs depended on the fact that the *Land* had become the world headquarters of Daimler-Benz, Porsche, Robert Bosch, and the European headquarters of Kodak and IBM. '*Tüfteln*' (widget-making) and its innovatory consequences resulted from the *Land* government encouraging multis to 'out-house' the production of components, as a means of massaging its *Mittelstand* supporters (artisans, shopkeepers and the self-employed) (Esser 1989: 100).

The 'Four Motors' were really a potentially intra-European, high-technology cartel. The regions which dominated the 'high-value-added' operations of the multis organised themselves collectively both to provide the infrastructure – higher education, technology transfer, high levels of public culture – that such firms required, and to resist threats to export production to low-wage countries. Baden-Württemberg was also the chief destination of incoming investment from the United Kingdom, itself the largest single investor in the Federal Republic in the 1980s. Its growth, funded by the proceeds of North Sea oil, was thus *at the expense* of UK regional development (Harvie 1992: 16).

This was a consciousness rooted in affluence, not in cultural identity. Cataluña had obvious linguistic and political distinctiveness, albeit that of the (Barcelona) city-region (Gallagher 1991: 124). Baden-Württemberg, like Rhône-Alpes, was culturally totally artificial. The three cultural communities of the 'South-Western State', only forty years old, extend across its boundaries: Franconia into Bavaria, Hesse and Thuringia; Swabia into Bavaria; and Allemania into Alsace and Switzerland – a cultural mix further complicated by post-war immigration, first from the east, then from Greece, Turkey and Jugoslavia, and the blurring of once-firm religious boundaries (Bausinger 1991: 28–31; Eschenburg 1991: 37–57).

Like Cataluña, Rhône-Alpes was the hinterland of a conurbation. 'Greater Lyons' was the major growth point of Gaullist France, with Lyons (thanks to the TGV) only two hours from Paris. In affluent Milan, the growth in the late 1980s of the Liga Lombarda under Umberto Bossi was more directed against Roman, and hence southern domination (seen as impoverished and corrupt) than a move towards positive civic and cultural identity. One factor that all the 'Motors' had in common was, in fact, a high quality of urban life plus an *absence* of the headquarters of major government or international bodies, such as were to be found in London, Brussels, Paris or Geneva. The observer of the *elites* of such regions would find something close to Adam Smith's ideal bourgeois – ideal in his derogations from *laissez-faire* as much as in his enterprise (Smith 1776, 1952: 318). As well as Pocock's affluent tourists, he might find new Metternichs, convinced that if the orient began on the Landstrasse, the Third World began on the Appian Way (Gallagher 1992).

THE LIMITS OF CIVIC VIRTUE

Within such regions, did the sort of virtue exist which could constrain the 'corruption' of wealth? This had contributed to the dissolution of the smaller polities, in the time of Hume and Smith, through the assault of commerce and the influence of the greater powers. The deficit in regional political culture and the density of civil society remained. 'If a city hasn't been used by an artist, not even the inhabitants live there imaginatively', wrote Alasdair Gray about Glasgow (Gray 1981, 1985: 243). But Glasgow's cultural and political identity was much firmer than that of most German provincial cities. In the former steel town of Bochum in the *Ruhrgebiet*, economic reorientation towards high-technology, higher education, and middlebrow entertainment – lavish productions of Andrew Lloyd Webber musicals – still left over 20,000 unemployed. Was this incipient 'downtown' underclass soon to be supplemented by redundant 'white-collar' workers, as computerisation gripped? In Geddes's terms, was the city now *neotechnic* for a majority – perhaps a bare majority – and *palaeotechnic* for the remainder? Events in Rostock in the summer of 1992 showed the ominous consequences which could stem from this.

Elsewhere, particularism continued in full flood. The timbre of Munich politics was still of Bavarian Catholic politicians intriguing away in their own hermetic world. Any loss of the Christian Social Union's privileged position in the Bonn government, or financial sacrifices to aid the 'red Protestants' of the East, would not be popular, and in 1990 the Minister-President even asked his law officers for an opinion on how Freistaat Bayern could leave the Bundesrepublik. This putative mutiny was overcome by the unexpected success of the CDU in the east, but could recur should the east revert politically to the left. The populist right, in the shape of Vaclav Klaus in the Czech republic, has already made one breakthrough. With Jörg Haider in Austria, it could make another. Given the success of Saarland-style cross-border arrangements, a conservative 'Alpine federation' (Bohemia, Bavaria, Austria, Switzerland, South Tyrol, Slovenia) – with its major bargaining-counter heavy investment in the control of Alpine trade routes – could indeed be on the cards.

More sinister was the fusion of regionalism with organised crime, which exploited those members of capitalist society whom multi-national capitalism had marginalised. Sicily had enjoyed a high degree of autonomy since the late 1940s, with an independent and unregulated banking system and the plentiful benefactions of the *Casa per il Mezzogiorno*. By the mid-1980s it was evident that this autonomy had been used to transform the Mafia into a global multinational dominated by and dominating the drugs trade, whose headquarters continued to be based on the island because of the protection which its politicians offered. With the assassination of the two leading legal officials mandated to curb the Mafia, it was evident that a challenge was being offered to the Italian state itself. Further corruption scandals disfigured the Socialist Party in northern Italy as well as the Mafia's traditional allies in the Christian Democrats, and showed how deeply it had impregnated the political culture of southern Italy. An analysis of private investment in the *Neuen Bundesländern* showed that laundered Mafia money was one of its main components. As industrial productivity gains left millions of young men marginalised as an 'underclass', and economic recovery failed to affect Russia and most of the former COMECON partners outwith the black market and arms trading, the potential for such business increased exponentially.

THE RISE AND FALL OF A REGIONALIST

Belgium in 1990 became the second – but probably not the last – member of the European Community to adopt a federal constitution (Monar 1993). So the German precedent appeared generally healthy. But was it? Matters did not remain tranquil for the inventor of the 'Four Motors'. From early 1989 onwards there had been revelations in Baden-Württemberg of the interpenetration of multinationals and the regional elite. The former Chairman of Bosch, Hans W. Merkle, was implicated in a slush fund operated for the benefit of the Baden-Württemberg CDU. Then the arrest of Helmut Lohr, the Chairman of SEL, a subsidiary of ITT (and Honorary UK Consul), on fraud and tax evasion charges, uncovered an elaborate system of payments to Lothar Späth: holidays, party donations, state visits abroad, in return for contracts and government subsidies. Späth was forced to resign early in January 1991, although he continued active as the Managing Director of the former state-owned Zeiss Kombinat in Jena in Saxony, Baden-Württemberg's 'partner-state' in the *Neuen Bundesländern*. The Späth case suggests the subordination of the elite to a disproportionately powerful capitalism: *tout court*, Adam Ferguson's 'corruption' (Born and Bertsch 1992).

Späth came to power in 1979 when his conservative predecessor, Hans Filbinger, was forced from office because of his Nazi past. Thus the 41-year-old meant a break with the German old order. As a non-university man, Swabian-speaking, and with a background in Lutheran church organisations, local administration and the trade-union-owned building concern Neue Heimat, Späth also represented a relatively consensual profile. During his period in office, he transformed the *Land*'s foreign relations in a way which first led to a challenge to Chancellor Kohl for the leadership of the Christian Democrat party in 1988. But, from the *Landtag*'s commission of inquiry, Späth appeared much less innovatory. The creation of a *Staatsministerium* enabled much of his activity to be hidden from parliamentary enquiry, while most of his cabinet were nonentities, assembled to balance the various factions of the CDU in the *Land*. His foreign visits were not just bankrolled with donations to CDU funds; they were masked by the government's officials and its legal department. Even after his fall, these scandals and manoeuvres continued, until desertions from the CDU to the far-right Republikaner party brought about the toppling of the last CDU-only *Land* regime in April 1992.

The case came at a bad time for the *Ländle*. The lack of regional planning had confined the 'economic miracle' to the Greater Stuttgart area; much of the south was under-industrialised and threatened by cutbacks in EC subsidies to agriculture. During Späth's premiership, road traffic had grown by 50 per cent (due in part to the 'just-in-time' assembly techniques of industry) and much of the Stuttgart area was persistently congested and smog-bound. Moreover, the unification of the country worked to the advantage of North Germany, North Rhine-Westphalia in particular. Baden-Württemberg was by 1993 in recession, like the rest of the West German economy only more so (with a 22 per cent fall in manufacturing industry in 1992–93), with its wonder-product, the motor car, in as deep disgrace as its former leader.

'SUCCESS: THREE YEARS IN THE LIFE OF A PROVINCE'

Ironically, the Grand Coalition saved Späth for another career. His Social Democrat critics took their ministries and held their fire, while a sceptical public looked on – or was diverted by the financial scandals which overtook Oskar Lafontaine in the Saarland as well as the Bavarian CSU in Munich. Was the power of 'bourgeois regionalism' in West Germany not the result of weakness – of its underlying civil society, which allowed too much autonomy to the political class; of the falling membership of established political parties; of the lack of that awkward concept, a German mission?

A particularly searing image of a self-obsessed elected political class was given in 1930 by the novelist Lion Feuchtwanger in *Success: Three Years in the Life of a Province* (Feuchtwanger 1930), set in Bavaria between 1921 and 1924. This was a remarkable and comprehensive portrait of the politics of Munich, at a time when Hitler, who briefly comes on the scene with his attempted *putsch*, was a marginal eccentric, like that Colonel Tejero who invaded the Spanish parliament in 1981. Feuchtwanger's Dr Klenk and Dr Bichler intrigue away, while inflation surges out of control and the forces of nationalism and antisemitism build up beyond the fringes of the Bavarian plateau.

A similar blend of the frightening and the parochial marked the three remarkable years which saw the unification of Germany: an object lesson, perhaps, in the inadequacies of 'co-operative federalism' when faced with a powerful challenge to adapt. Helmut Kohl, who resembled Bismarck in no other respect, had the gift A.J.P. Taylor attributed to the latter – of intriguing himself into impossible situations, and then spectacularly releasing himself. The neurotic Prussian reactionary and the phlegmatic Rhineland party hatchet-man united Germany for reasons which had little to do with nationalism but a lot to do with regional politics, suddenly played out on a far larger scale. In Kohl's case, this was largely through the weakness of his own party. In his book *The German Right*, the Social Democrat politician Peter Glotz pointed to the atrophying of the local society of carnival association, *Stammtisch*, and chamber of commerce which had traditionally under-pinned the CDU (Glotz 1986). The wealthy were opting for a 'privatised' lifestyle. The younger generation were moving either to the Greens (if academically educated) or to the 'radical right' Republikaner (if averagely qualified and insecure). The *Gastarbeiter* (guest workers) were disqualified from political participation. The successor generation seemed to have fallen away completely (Glotz 1986: 106). This weakness hit Bavaria after the death in 1988 of Franz-Josef Strauss and Baden-Württemberg after the fall of Späth. Financial scandals dogged the CDU in one *Land* election after another – 'dirty tricks' and the suicide of the Prime Minister, Rainer Barschel, in Schleswig Holstein; brothels in Hesse; casinos in Lower Saxony – with unpleasant consequences for those Bonn politicians who had also a regional status.

In early 1989, when 'real existing socialism' still looked unchallenged, this fate befell Kohl's rival Gerhard Stoltenberg. Nailed as partly responsible for the events leading to the Barschel scandal, he lost his post as Finance Minister to the Bavarian Theo Waigel, making the centre-right coalition more dependent both on the Liberal FDP, and on the Bavarian CSU. Under two 'Easterners', Hans-Dietrich Genscher and Count Otto Lambsdorff, the Liberals had always favoured German unity and 'market forces'. The CSU had also run its own *Ostpolitik*, bankrolling the old DDR for years, with Strauss regarded as being uncomfortably close to the Stasi, through the trading connections of some of his party colleagues. Now it was worried about the far right drifting to the Republikaner, which it promptly did, and – when the Wall fell in November – about the 'Red Prussian' input into an enlarged Bundesrepublik, which would gravely diminish its traditional privileged role in the West German right (making up about a quarter of any federal cabinet).

So the CSU leaped into East German politics, founding its own sister party, the Deutsche Soziale Union. The CDU had to follow it, even at the cost of alliance with the *Blockflöten* (East German communist stooges) of the old East CDU. This seemed superfluous, because the polls showed the ex-DDR about to vote at its first – and only – national elections solidly on the left. The CDU exerted itself because it expected to be crushed, then suddenly realised that an emotional revulsion against the word 'socialism' and its own 'swap your Trabbi for a Merc' propaganda, had made it the favourite. Kohl, landing at Leipzig Airport, saw the crowds and remarked to his Interior Minister, Schäuble: 'Es ist gelaufen' ('It's running our way'). The CDU ended up an almost baffled victor, capturing every one of the new *Länder* with the exception of Berlin and Brandenburg, and placed in Kohl's trembling hands the chance of becoming first Chancellor of German unity. He took it.

Kohl's honeymoon was brief. A Catholic Rhineland politician in the mould of Adenauer, he had no real interest in East Germany and never visited the place for over six months after his Bundestag victory in December 1990. *And no one noticed.* Friction between *Wessis* (West Germans) and *Ossis* (East Germans), the rise of neo-Nazism among the unemployed and directionless youth, the continuing problems of the East German economy: these eroded CDU support in the East, while the SPD dominated the rich Western *Länder* without evolving a Bonn leadership strong enough to take Kohl on. But most *West* German voters – beyond visits to Berlin, and bus-tours for elderly day-trippers – took minimal interest in the *Neuen Bundesländer*. Goethe's notion of the 'elective nationality' of the Germans was borne out by their affinity to Tuscany or Ireland; *Ossis* validly complained that they felt even more remote from the West than before 1989, and in 1992 formed a 'solidarity' campaign – dominated by former, albeit dissident, communists – to express this view (Enzensberger 1989; Stares 1992).

Germany in the 1990s is not a putative West European superpower, as in the imaginings of Conor Cruise O'Brien or the Thatcher Cabinet at its famous Chequers seance. A nation reunited by provincial politicians pursuing provincial ends has emerged an introverted state whose capacity for cohesion has been significantly diminished. Its political class, Social Democrat as well as conservative, restricted by the boundaries of its *Länder*, has been tried and found wanting. As it has the best developed system of feeding regional opinion into the decision-making processes of the European Community, this is, at least in the medium term, serious.

FOG IN CHANNEL: CONTINENT CUT OFF

So how do we assess the claims of the 'positive' and 'negative' accounts? I have dwelt perhaps overlong on the shadow side, which seems most identified with the right: it is perhaps a pessimistic account because, in comparison with Britain, the German right – Späth included – has for much of the time acted in a responsible and consensual manner. If such men cannot stand up to the pressure of 'corruption', or take a more European perspective, what about their counterparts in political cultures which have less virtue? Can small mean secretive and unstatesmanlike? If nation-state Europe has lately produced few politicians who rival the moral status of de Gaulle or Brandt, regional leaderships have lacked any significant profile. If political communities require their constitutions to have Bagehot's 'dignified parts', then the nation-state has still produced its Walesas, Weizsäckers and Mary Robinsons, while 'Europe' and its regions remain anonymous.

But – who is President of Switzerland? Who is *Prime Minister* of Switzerland? Happy is the country which has no need of 'dignified parts'? Regionalism, in its modest way, has shown many positive elements. The German *Länder* provide a reservoir of federal ministers who know what governing is like, unlike the situation in the British Labour party. However lethargic they can be with regard to educational policy, at least German academics can regard themselves as on occasion beneficiaries and *authorities*, and not as victims. The Green party, which made an unholy mess of its political career in Bonn, now forms a part of four *Land* ministries, with appreciable results in terms of environment, transport and civil rights policies. Partly as a result of the sort of pressure it represents, women have now taken on a much greater profile in German political life, with 40 per cent representation now a rule in SPD ministries. Above all, new means of democracy, initiative referenda and the encouragement of citizens' action groups, are now making good the deficiencies in civil society: proposals for gaining *Ausländer* (non-German residents) the local government vote came from the SPD *Länder*, not from Bonn (Marsh 1989: 280–97).

It is obvious that modifications, in European Community structure, regional and intra-European organisation, and European political culture, can draw on the German experience – particularly that of the Bundesrat in monitoring EC legislation – and thus inhibit the decline of regionalism into a 'particularism of the affluent': but the risk is there (Bulmer 1986: 256ff.). Combatting it seems particularly the task of the European left, whose record in this area appears to have improved. The 'national history' which Pocock sees in eclipse was essentially the possession of the same bourgeoisie that compromised with the dynasties and the right. Perhaps the demotic moralism of 1968 – of which the growth of labour, regional and minority history was an important part – wasn't wasted, after all, and ought now to take its chance.

Which brings us finally to our own wobbly vantage-point: region and nation within the United Kingdom, now the last large-scale centralised state in Europe. Regional identity remains politically vague in England, but positive, not to say aggressive, in Scotland, Wales and Northern Ireland. The continuing surrender of regional bourgeois elites to the capital concentrations of the City of London ran, in the 1980s, into the buffers of congestion, inflated costs and an under-financed infrastructure. The ability of Scotland, Wales and (with inevitable reservations) Northern Ireland to balance this with the accumulation of devolved administrative powers was not available to the English regions, from which the Thatcher government removed such planning powers as remained and the 'city-region' structures of the metropolitan counties (Davids, Krause and Metscher 1992: 64–71). The attempt by the Major government to purchase SNP support for Maastricht by promising the Scots a fifth of the UK seats on the Committee of the Regions showed an attitude to English regionalism which was, at least, cavalier.

Yet the paradox was that the concept of the region as an administrative unit remained. Even within England, some regions have a more power-ful cultural presence than *Länder* in West Germany, as the Kilbrandon Report (along with other inquiries into local government) showed in the 1970s (Birch 1977: 151–66; Harvie 1991: 105–18). Thatcherism in a sense relied on the patience of a densely organised civil society to hold the community together while it perverted English nationalism into a sort of dystopic regionalism: a Senate of Nimbyia governing an initially privileged south-east, unplanned and unbound by any political loyalties. The consequences of this experience – a collapsing transport structure and the economic catastrophe of the London office property market – produced first the raucous nationalism of Essex Man, and then a paranoia about what the entry to Europe might entail. After the Maastricht Treaty, the Scots and Welsh looked coolly on while politicians from the region which was indubitably part of the European core – and desperately dependent on being recognised as such – twisted themselves into a nationalistic fervour which would have been horrify-ing had it come from Germans.

Sir Peter Ustinov once remarked that this English neurosis was all the stranger, since several centuries of union – and union of a very centralising sort – within the British Isles had failed to diminish the separate identity of Scotland, Wales or Ireland. The natural regionality of the British Isles – the persistence of distinct national traditions and the comparative strength of civil society – could be of enormous value to a federated Europe, while the assertion of a 'British' identity by Conservative politicians such as Lady Thatcher and Lord Tebbitt smacks more of a lack of confidence about the identity and competence of the British state. The value of the British tradition lies in disseminating sovereignty within the British nations and, simultaneously, injecting the strengths of their civil society into the creaky and over-formal structures of an evolving European polity, or it lies nowhere at all.

References

Note: The abbreviation *CS* stands for *Comparative Studies on Governments and Non-Dominant Ethnic Groups in Europe, 1850–1940*, Aldershot: European Science Foundation/New York University Press/Dartmouth. Volumes published to date include: **1** J.J. Tomiak (ed.) (1991) *Schooling, Educational Policy and Ethnic Identity*; **2** Donal A. Kerr (ed.) (1992) *Religion, State and Ethnic Groups*; **5** Paul Smith (ed.) (1991) *Ethnic Groups in International Relations*; **6** Andreas Kappeler (ed.) (1992) *The Formation of National Elites*. Volumes to come: **3** Sergij Vilfan (ed.) (1993) *Ethnic Groups and Langauage Rights*; **4** Geoffrey Alderman (ed.) (1993) *Governments, Ethnic Groups and Political Representation*; **7** David Howell (ed.) (1993) *Roots of Rural Ethnic Mobilisation*; **8** Max Engman (ed.) (1992) *Ethnic Identity in Urban Europe*.

Acton, Lord (1862, 1907) 'Nationality', in *The History of Freedom and Other Essays*, London: Macmillan.
Acton, Edward (1992) 'State and society under Lenin and Stalin', in P. Hayes *Themes in Modern European History 1890–1945*, London: Routledge.
Anderson, Benedict (1983) *Imagined Communities*, London: Verso.
Anderson, Olive (1967) *A Liberal State at War*, London: Macmillan.
Anderson, Robert D. (1975) *Education in France, 1848–1870*, Oxford: Oxford University Press.
Annan, Noel (1958) 'The intellectual aristocracy', in J.H. Plumb (ed.) *Studies in Social History*, London: Longman.
Ara, Angelo (1991) 'Italian educational policy towards national minorities, 1860–1940', in *CS*, 1, 263–90.
Ardagh, John (1979) *A Tale of Five Cities: Life in Europe Today*, New York: Harper & Row.
—— (1982, 1986) *France in the 1980s*, Harmondsworth: Penguin.
Arnold, Matthew (1868) *Schools and Universities on the Continent*, London: Macmillan.
—— (1867, 1912) *The Study of Celtic Literature*, London: Smith Elder.
Ashford, Douglas (1982) *British Dogmatism and French Pragmatism: Centre–Local Relations in the Welfare State*, London: Allen & Unwin.
Ashton, Rosemary (1986, 1989) *Little Germany: German Refugees in Victorian Britain*, Oxford: Oxford University Press.
Aspinwall, Bernard (1980) *Portable Utopia: Glasgow and the United States*, Aberdeen: Aberdeen University Press.

—— (1982) 'David Urquhart, Robert Monteith and the Catholic Church: A search for justice and peace', *The Innes Review*, 57–70.

Barker, Ernest (1915) *Political Thought from Spencer to Today*, London: Williams & Norgate.

Bausinger, Hermann (ed.) (1983) *Heitere Gefühle bei der Ankunft auf dem Lande: Bilder schwäbischen Landlebens im 19. Jahrhundert*, Tübingen: Ludwig-Uhland-Institut.

—— (1991) 'Political Culture in Baden-Württemberg', in H.U. Wehling (ed.) *The German Southwest*, Stuttgart: Kohlhammer, 17–36.

Berg, Maxine (1985) *The Age of Manufactures*, Cambridge: Cambridge University Press.

Berghahn, Volker (1988) 'The American influence on post-war German industry', unpublished lecture delivered at the Goethe Institute, London.

Best, Geoffrey (1980) *Humanity in Warfare*, London: Weidenfeld & Nicolson.

Biagini, Eugenio F. (1992) *Liberty, Retrenchment and Reform: Popular Liberalism in the Age of Gladstone, 1860–1880*, Cambridge: Cambridge University Press.

Biddiss, Michael D. (1970) *Father of Racist Ideology: Arthur de Gobineau*, London: Weidenfeld & Nicholson.

Birch, Anthony (1977) *Political Integration and Disintegration in the British Isles*, London: Allen & Unwin.

Bjorn, C. (1993) 'Germans and Danes', in Alexander Grant and Keith Stringer (eds) *The Formation of Social Identities in the European Past*, Copenhagen: Copenhagen University Press.

Blaschke, Jochen (1980) *Handbuch der westeuropäischen Regionalbewegungen*, Frankfurt: Syndikat.

Bluntschli, Johann Kaspar (1871) *Europa als Staatenbund*, Bonn.

Boelcke, Willi (1987) *Wirtschaftsgeschichte Baden-Württembergs*, Stuttgart: Konrad Theiss Verlag.

Bogdanor, Vernon (1977) 'Regionalism: The constitutional aspects', *Political Quarterly* (April–June), 164–70.

Borchardt, Knut (1973) 'Germany', in Carlo M. Cipolla (ed.) *The Fontana Economic History of Europe*, 4.1., London: Collins, 76–160.

Born, Martin and Benno Bertsch (1992) *Die Maultaschen-Connection*, Göttingen: Steidl.

Boyle, Kevin (1988) 'The Anglo-Irish Agreement, 1985: differing perceptions, differing realities', in W.J. Allan Macartney (ed.), *Self-Determination in the Commonwealth*, Aberdeen: Aberdeen University Press, 91–9.

Bramke, Werner (1993) 'Die Industrieregion Sachsen', in R. Schulze *Structural Change in Early Industrialised Regions*, Essen: Klartext Verlag.

Braudel, Fernand (1949) *The Mediterranean*, London: Collins.

—— (1979, 1985) *Civilisation and Capitalism*, 1: *The Structures of Everyday Life* , New York: Harper & Row.

—— (1988) *The Identity of France*, 1: *History and Environment*, London: Collins.

Briggs, Asa (1958) *The Age of Improvement*, London: Longmans.

—— (1963, 1968) *Victorian Cities*, Harmondsworth: Pelican.

Brunn, Gerhard (1992) 'The Catalans within the Spanish monarchy from the middle of the nineteenth to the beginning of the twentieth century', in *CS*, 6, 133–59.

Bryce, James (1922) *Modern Democracies*, London: Macmillan.

Brzezinski, Zbigniew (1989) 'Post-Communist nationalism', *Foreign Affairs*, 68, II, 1–25.

Bullmann, Udo (ed.) (1993) *Die Regionen im EG-Integrationsprozess*, Giessen: Nomos.

Bulmer, Simon John (1986) *The Domestic Structure of European Community Policy-Making in West Germany*, London: Garland.

Bulmer, Simon John and William Paterson (1987) *The Federal Republic of Germany and the European Community*, London: Allen & Unwin.

Bulpitt, James (1983) *Territory and Power in the United Kingdom*, Manchester: Manchester University Press.

Burgess, Michael (ed.) (1986) *Federalism and Federation in Western Europe*, London: Croom Helm.

Business International (1986) *Europe Inc.*, London: Business International.

Byrd, Peter (1980) *The International Environment for Territorial Politics in the United Kingdom*, Glasgow: Strathclyde University, Centre for the Study of Public Policy.

Calder, Angus (1969, 1971) *The People's War*, London: Granada.

Chalmers, Thomas (1821–6) *The Christian and Civic Economy of Great Towns*, 3 vols, Glasgow: Chalmers & Collins.

Checkland, Sidney (1980) 'The British city-region as historical and political challenge', in Sidney Pollard (ed.) *Region und Industrialisierung*, Göttingen.

Clarke, P.F. (1971) *Lancashire and the New Liberalism*, Cambridge: Cambridge University Press.

Clogg, Richard (1983) *Greece in the 1980s*, London: Macmillan.

Clout, Hugh D. (ed.) (1987) *Regional Development in Europe*, London: David Fulton.

Cochrane, Allan (1993) 'Creating a planning region', in U. Bullmann (ed.) *Die Regionen in EG-Integrationsprozess*, Giessen: Giessen University Press.

Coleman, William D. and Henry J. Jacek (1989) *Regionalism, Business Interests and Public Policy*, London: Sage.

Colletis, Georges (1993) 'Region Rhône-Alpes', in U. Bullmann (ed.) *Die Regionen im EG-Integrationsprozess*, Giessen: University Press.

Colley, Linda (1984) 'Whose nation? Class and national consciousness in Britain, 1750–1830', *Past and Present*, 113, 97–117.

—— (1992) *Britons*, Cambridge, Mass.: Yale University Press.

Compagna, Francesco and Calogero Muscara (1980) 'Regionalism and social change in Italy', in Jean Gottmann, *Centre and Periphery*, London: Sage, 101–6.

Cooke, Philip and Kevin Morgan (1990) 'Baden-Württemberg – A growth region for Wales to emulate?', Cardiff: University of Wales, Department of City and Regional Planning.

—— (1991) 'Learning through Networking: Baden-Württemberg and the New Industrial Order', Cardiff: University of Wales, Department of City and Regional Planning.

Coombes, David (1991) 'Europe and the regions', in B. Crick (ed.) *National Identities: the Constitution of the United Kingdom*, Oxford: *Political Quarterly*/Blackwell, 134–50.

Council of Europe (1986) *Role of the Regions in Building Europe*, Strasbourg: Office of the Council.

Craig, Gordon A. (1991) *The Germans*, Harmondsworth: Penguin.

Crick, Bernard (ed.) (1991) *National Identities: the Constitution of the United Kingdom*, Oxford: *Political Quarterly*/ Blackwell.

Crouch, Colin and David Marquand (eds) (1989) *The New Centralism: Britain out of Step in Europe?*, Oxford: Blackwell.

Crouzet, François (1966, 1968) 'England and France in the eighteenth century: a comparative analysis of two economic growths', translated by A. Sondheimer, in Max Hartwell (ed.) *The Causes of the Industrial Revolution*, London: Methuen, 139–73.

Cunningham, Hugh (1975) *The Volunteer Force*, London: Croom Helm.

Dahrendorf, Ralf (1984) *On Britain*, London: BBC Publications.

Daunton, M.J. (1977) *Coal Metropolis: Cardiff, 1870–1914*, Leicester: Leicester University Press.

Davids, Jens-Ulrich, Delia Krause and Priscilla Metscher (eds) (1992) *Britische Regionen, oder: Wie einheitlich ist das Königreich?*, Gulliver Deutsch-Englische Jahrbücher Band 31, Hamburg: Argument.

Davie, George Elder (1961) *The Democratic Intellect: Scotland and her Universities in the Nineteenth Century*, Edinburgh: Edinburgh University Press.

—— (1971) *The Scottish Enlightenment and Other Essays*, Edinburgh: Polygon.

Day, Graham and Gareth Rees (eds) (1991) *Regions, Nations and European Integration: Remaking the Celtic Periphery*, Cardiff: University of Wales Press.

Denton, Geoffrey (1983) 'Regional problems and policy in the EEC', in Roy Jenkins (ed.) *Britain and The EEC*, London: Macmillan, 72–85.

Dicey, Albert Venn (1905, 1963) *Law and Public Opinion in England During the Nineteenth Century*, London: Macmillan.

Dickinson, Robert E. (1967) *The City-Region in Western Europe*, London: Routledge.

Donaldson, William (1986) *Popular Literature in Victorian Scotland: Language, Fiction and the Press*, Aberdeen: Aberdeen University Press.

Dorondo, D.R. (1992) *Bavaria and German Federalism*, London: St Martin's Press.

Earle, John (1975) *Italy in the 1970s*, London: David & Charles.

Edwards, A.W.J. (1978) 'Technical Education and the "Zweiter Bildungsweg"', in Arthur Hearnden (ed.) *The British in Germany*, London: Hamilton, 174–97.

Ehrlich, Carola (1988) 'The "Dialectable Duchy": regionalism in the novels of Sir Arthur Thomas Quiller-Couch', Tübingen: unpublished MA dissertation.

Eliot, T.S. (1948) *Notes Towards the Definition of Culture*, London: Faber.

Elkar, Rainer S. (1981) *Europas unruhige Regionen*, Stuttgart: Klett.

Ellger, Christof (1983) 'The Spatial Distribution of the Information Technology Industry in Baden-Württemberg', Tübingen: unpublished MA dissertation.

Emsley, Clive (1983) *Policing and its Context*, London: Macmillan.

Endemann, Fritz (1991) 'The structure of administration in Baden-Württemberg', in H.U. Wehling (ed) *The German Southwest*, Stuttgart: Kohlhammer, 97–120.

Enzensberger, Hans-Magnus (1989) *Europe! Europe!*, London: Radius.

Eriksen, Knut, Andreas Kazamias, Robin Okey and J.J. Tomiak (1991) 'Governments and the education of non-dominant ethnic groups in comparative perspective', in *CS*, 1, 389–417.

Eschenburg, Theodor (1991) 'The formation of the state of Baden-Württemberg', in H.U. Wehling (ed) *The German Southwest*, Stuttgart: Kohlhammer, 37–57.

Esser, Josef (1989) 'Does industrial policy matter? Land governments in research and technology policy in federal Germany', in C. Crouch and D. Marquand, (eds) *The New Centralism*, Oxford: Blackwell, 94–108.

Evans, R.J.W. (1992) 'Frontiers and national identities in Central Europe', *The International History Review*, XIV, 3 (August), 481–98.

Eyck, Frank (1968) *The Frankfurt Parliament, 1848–1849*, London: Macmillan.

Fair, John D. (1980) *British Interparty Conferences*, Oxford: Clarendon.

Fawcett, C.B. (1921) *The Provinces of England*, London: Williams and Norgate.

Fayat, Hendrick (1990) 'Benelux', in René Bryssinck (ed.) *Modern Belgium*, Brussels: Modern Belgium Association, 108–40.

Ferguson, Adam (1767, 1966) *An Essay on the History of Civil Society*, Edinburgh: Edinburgh University Press.

Feuchtwanger, Lion (1930) *Success: Three Years in the Life of a Province*, translated by Edwin and Willa Muir, London: Martin Secker.

Fietz, Lothar, Paul Hoffmann and Hans-Werner Ludwig (eds) (1982) *Regionalität, Nationalität und Internationalität in der zeitgenössischen Lyrik*, Tübingen: Attempto.

Fisher, H.A.L. (1927) *Life of James Bryce, Viscount Bryce of Dechmont*, London: Macmillan.

Fitzmaurice, James (1981) *Politics in Denmark*, London: Hurst.

Forbes, Duncan (1952) *The Liberal Anglican Idea of History*, Cambridge: Cambridge University Press.

Foster, Roy (1988) *Modern Ireland, 1600–1972*, London: Allen Lane.

Freeze, Gregory (1990) 'New scholarship on the Russian peasantry', in *European History Quarterly*.

Gallagher, Tom (1987) *The Uneasy Peace*, Manchester: Manchester University Press.

—— (1991) 'Autonomy in Spain: lessons for Britain?', in B. Crick, *National Identities*, Oxford: *Political Quarterly*/Blackwell, 119–33.

—— (1992) 'Rome at bay: the challenge of the Northern League to the Italian state', *Government and Opposition*, vol.27, no.4, autumn.

García, Eusebio Gonzales (1983) 'Autonomy and control of "Local Corporations", *Journal of Regional Policy*, 4.

Garrido, José Luís García (1991) 'Spanish educational policy and non-dominant ethnic groups', in *CS*, 1, 293–318.

Geddes, Patrick (1915) *Cities in Evolution*, London: Williams & Norgate.

Geo Spezial: Baden-Württemberg (1985) Hamburg: Gruner & Jahr.

Gerdes, Dirk (ed.) (1980) *Aufstand der Provinz: Regionalismus in Westeuropa*, New York: Campus.

Gerdes, Dirk and Roland Sturm (1987) *Regionen und Regionalismus in Westeuropa*, Stuttgart: Kohlhammer.

Geyer, Michael (1987) 'The Nazi-state reconsidered', in R. Bessell (ed.) *Life in the Third Reich*, Oxford: Oxford University Press.

Giddens, Anthony (1984) *The Constitution of Society*, London: Polity Press.

Glotz, Peter (1986) *Die deutsche Rechte*, Stuttgart: DVA.

Gottmann, Jean (1980) *Centre and Periphery*, London: Sage.

80   *The Rise of Regional Europe*

Graham, David and Peter Clarke (1985) *The New Enlightenment*, London: Macmillan.
Gramsci, Antonio (1971) *Prison Notebooks*, London: Lawrence & Wishart.
Gray, Alasdair (1981, 1985) *Lanark*, Edinburgh: Canongate.
Green, David G. (1981) *Power and Party in an English City: An Account of Single-Party Rule*, London: Allen & Unwin.
Greiner, Bernard (1992) 'Räpresentation und Dezentrierung: Aspekte des Regionalismus in der deutschen literarischen Tradition' in Fietz and Ludwig, (eds) *Regionalität, Nationalität und Internationalität in der Zeitgenössischen Lyrik*, Tübingen: Attempto, 83–92.
Gyford, John (1980) 'Socialism and decentralisation: dilemmas and ambiguities', London: Fabian Society, unpublished paper.
Hahn, Ottokar (1988) unpublished address to International Forum of Scottish Council: Development and Industry.
Haldane, Richard Burdon (1902) *Education and Empire*, London: Murray.
Hanna, William (ed.) (1877) *Letters of Thomas Erskine of Linlathen*, Edinburgh: David Douglas.
Hardie, Jeremy (1975) 'Regional policy', in Wilfred Beckermann (ed.), *The Labour Government's Economic Record, 1964–1970*, London: Duckworth, 218–46.
Harrison, Frederic (1905) *John Ruskin*, London: Macmillan.
Harvie, Christopher (1976) 'Ideology and home rule: James Bryce, A.V. Dicey and Ireland, 1880–1887', *English Historical Review*, XCI, 359 (April), 298–314.
—— (1977) *Scotland and Nationalism, 1907–1977*, London: Allen & Unwin.
—— (1983) 'Scott and the image of Scotalnd', in Alan Bold (ed.) *Sir Walter Scott: The Lond-Forgotten Melody*, London: Vision Books.
—— (1988) 'The politics of German railway design', *Journal of Design History*, I, 3–4, 235–47.
—— (1989) 'Dicey's last stand', in Colin Crouch and David Marquand (eds), *The New Centralism: Britain out of Step in Europe?*, Oxford: Blackwell, 39–55.
—— (1990a) 'Gladstonianism, the provinces, and popular political culture', in Richard Bellamy (ed.) *Victorian Liberalism*, London: Methuen, 152–74.
—— (1990b) 'Yes, Minister-President!', *Planet*, 79 (Feb–March).
—— (1991) 'English regionalism: the dog that never barked', in Bernard Crick (ed.) *National Identities*, Oxford: *Political Quarterly*/ Blackwell, 105–119.
—— (1992) 'Confessions of a bourgeois regionalist', unpublished talk given to the Social History Society, Glasgow.
Haycraft, John (1987) *Italian Labyrinth*, Harmondsworth: Penguin.
Hayes, Paul (1992) *Themes in Modern European History, 1890–1945*, London: Routledge.
Headlam-Morley, Alice (1928) *The New Democratic Constitutions of Europe*, Oxford: Oxford University Press.
Hechter, Michael (1975) *Internal Colonialism: The Celtic Fringe in British National Development*, London: Routledge.
Hitler, Adolf (1925–7, 1939) *Mein Kampf*, trans James Murphy, London: Allen and Unwin.
Hoffmann, Erich (1992) 'The role of institutions of higher and secondary learning', in *CS*, 6, 277–92.

Holton, Robert (1986) *Cities, Capitalism and Civilisation*, London: Allen & Unwin.

Janik, Allan and Stephen Toulmin (1973) *Wittgenstein's Vienna*, London: Simon & Schuster.

Janowitz, Morris (1957, 1968) 'Military elites and the study of war', in Leon Bramson and George W. Goethals (eds) *War: Studies from Psychology, Sociology, Anthropology*, New York: Basic Books, 344–57.

Jarvie, Grant and Graham Walker (1993) *Scottish Sport in the Making of the Nation*, Leicester: Leicester University Press.

Jenkins, Brian and Gunter Minnerup (1985) *Citizens and Comrades: Socialism in a World of Nation States*, London: Pluto Press.

Johnston, R.J. (ed.) (1988) *Nationalism, Self-Determination and Political Geography*, London: Croom Helm.

Joll, James (1971) *Anarchism Today*, London: Macmillan.

Jones, George (1969) *Borough Politics*, London: Macmillan.

Kappeler, Andreas (1992) 'National organisations', in *CS*, 6, 293–307.

Kazamias, Andreas (1991) 'The education of the Greeks in the Ottoman Empire, 1856–1923: a case-study of "controlled toleration"', in *CS*, 1, 344–67.

Keating, Michael (1988) *State and Regional Nationalism: Territorial Politics and the Regional State*, Hemel Hempstead: Wheatsheaf.

—— (1991) 'Nations, regions and international regimes', Newcastle: UK Politics Workgroup, unpublished paper.

Keting, Michael and M. Rhodes (1983) 'Is there a regional level of government in England?', Glasgow: Centre for the Study of Public Policy.

Kendle, J.E. (1968) 'The Round Table movement and "home rule all round"', *The Historical Journal*, XI, 2, 332–53.

Kerr, Donal A. (1992) 'Religion, state and ethnic identity', in *CS*, 2, 1–26.

King, Russell (1987) *Italy*, London: Harper and Row.

Kleinknecht, Thomas (1985) *Imperiale und internationale Ordnung: eine Untersuchung zum Gelehrtenliberalismus am Beispiel von James Bryce, 1838–1922*, Göttingen: Vandenhoeck und Rupprecht.

Kloss, Günther (1976, 1982) *West Germany: An Introduction*, London: Macmillan.

Kohr, Leopold (1975) *The Breakdown of Nations*, London: Routledge.

—— (1941, 1991) 'Einigung durch Teilung', *Die Zeit* (18 October 1991).

Kropotkin, Prince Peter (1942) *Kropotkin: Selections from his Writings*, ed. Herbert Read, London: Freedom Press.

Lafontaine, Oskar (1989) 'Mehr Macht für Europas Regionen', *Geo*, 4 (April), 210–11; unpublished translation by C. Ehrlich.

Land Baden-Württemberg (1991) *Eine kleine politische Landeskunde*, Stuttgart: Landeszentrale für politische Bildung.

Lane, Christel (1990) 'Vocational training and new production concepts in the FRG: some lessons for Britain', *Industrial Relations Journal*, XXI, 4 (Winter), 247–56.

Langer, William L. (1969) *Political and Social Upheaval*, New York: Harper & Row.

Léclaire, Lucien (1954) *Le Roman Régionaliste dans les Iles Britanniques, 1800–1950*, Clermont-Ferrand: Debussac.

Lenman, Robin (1990) 'Art and tourism in southern Germany, 1850–1930', in Arthur Marwick (ed.) *The Arts, Literature and Society*, London: Routledge, 163–80.

82   *The Rise of Regional Europe*

Leruez, Jacques (1975) *Economic Planning and Politics in Britain*, London: Martin Robertson.
—— (1983) *Ecosse: Une nation sans état*, Lille: Presses Universitaires.
Linklater, Magnus and Robin Denniston (eds) (1992) *Anatomy of Scotland*, Edinburgh: Chambers.
Lorimer, James (1872, 1880) *The Institutes of Law*, Edinburgh: Murray.
—— (1884) *The Institutes of the Law of Nations*, Edinburgh: Murray.
Ludwig, Klemens (1991) *Baltikum*, Munich: Beck'sche Reihe.
—— (1992) *Europa zerfällt*, Reinbek: Rowohlt.
Maastricht Treaty of European Union (7 February 1992) Article 198a.
McAllister, R. (1980) *Local Government: Death or Devolution?*, London: Outer Circle Policy Unit.
MacDonald, J.F. (1979) *The Lack of Political Identity in English Regions*, Glasgow: Centre for the Study of Public Policy.
MacDonald, M. (1989) *We are not French! Language, Culture and Identity in Brittany*, London: Routledge.
Machin, Howard (1977) *The Prefect in French Public Administration*, London: Croom Helm.
MacKay, R.W.G. (1940) *Federal Union*, London: Allen & Unwin.
McKibbin, Ross (1974) *The Evolution of the Labour Party, 1907–1924*, Oxford: Oxford University Press.
Mackinder, Halford (1919) *Democratic Ideas and Reality*, London: Constable.
Mackintosh, J.P. (1974) 'The Royal Commission on the Constitution, 1969–1973', *Political Quarterly* (January-March), 115–18.
Marsh, David (1992) *Germany at the Crossroads*, London: Radius.
Marshall, J.D. (ed.) (1977) *The History of Lancashire County Council, 1889–1974*, London: Martin Robertson.
Mayo, Patricia Elton (1974) *The Roots of Identity: Three National Movements in Contemporary European Politics*, London: Allen Lane.
Meller, Helen (1973) 'Patrick Geddes: an analysis of his theory of civics, 1880–1904', in *Victorian Studies*.
—— (1976) *Leisure and the Changing City, 1870–1914*, London: Routledge.
—— (1990) *Patrick Geddes: Social Evolutionist and City Planner*, London: Routledge.
Mendels, Franklin F. (1972) 'Proto-industrialisation', *Journal of Economic History*, 32, 241–61.
Mester, Bernd (1985) 'Partikularismus der Schiene: Die Entwicklung einzel-staatlicher Eisenbahnsysteme bis 1870', in Deutsche Bundesbahn, *Zug der Zeit*, Munich: Orbis, 196–205.
Middlemass, Robert Keith (1965) *The Clydesiders*, London: Hutchinson.
Milne, Alasdair (1988) *D.G.: The Memoirs of a British Broadcaster*, London: Hodder & Stoughton.
Milward, Alan S. (1984) *The Reconstruction of Western Europe*, London: Routledge.
—— (1992) *The European Rescue of the Nation State*, London: Routledge.
Modeen, Tore (1991) 'The Åland Islands Question', in *CS*, 5, 153–68.
Monar, Joerg (1993) 'Die Rolle der Belgischen "Gemeinschaften" und "Regionen" im Bereich der Auswärtigen Beziehungen: Ein Modell für die Zukünftige Europäische Union?', in U. Bullmann, *Die Regionen im EG-Integrationsprozess*, Giessen: Giessen University Press.

Mowat, R.B. (1966) *Ruin and Resurgence, 1939–1965*, London: Blandford.

Myhre, Jan Eivind (1988) 'Nordic urban history and urban historians in the last decade', *Urban History Yearbook*, 65–9.

Nairn, Tom (1977) *The Break-up of Britain*, London: Verso.

—— (1988) *The Enchanted Glass: Britain and its Monarchy*, London: Radius.

—— (1991) 'Viewing Europe: the undiscovered country', Glasgow: Scottish Television, unpublished programme paper.

Nicholls, David (1973) *Pluralist Political Theory in Britain*, London: Allen & Unwin.

Osmond, John and Angela Graham (1984) *Alternatives*, Wellingborough: Thorsons.

Oxford English Dictionary: Supplementary Volume (1982), Oxford: Oxford University Press.

Page, Edward C. (1991) *Localism and Centralism in Europe*, Oxford: Oxford Unversity Press.

—— (1993) 'The future of local government in Britain', in U. Bullmann (ed.) *Die Regionen im EG-Integrationsprozess*, Giessen: Giessen University Press.

Palm, E. (1993) 'The Berg region of Sweden' in R. Schulze (ed.) *Structural Change in Early Industrialised Regions*, Essen: Klartext Verlag.

Paxton, John (1984) *A Dictionary of the European Communities*, London: Macmillan.

Payne, Peter L. (1974) *British Entrepreneurship in the Nineteenth Century*, London: Allen & Unwin.

Peters, B. Guy (1991) *European Politics Reconsidered*, New York: Holmes & Meier.

Petzina, Dietmar (1993) 'Von der industriellen Führungsregion zum Krisengebiet: Das Ruhrgebiet in historischer Perspektive', in R. Schulze (ed.) *Structural Change in Early-Industrialised Regions*, Essen: Klartext Verlag.

Phillipson, Nicholas (1968) 'Nationalism and Ideology', in J.N. Wolfe (ed.) *Government and Nationalism in Scotland*, Edinburgh: Edinburgh University Press, 167–88.

Picht, Georg (ed.) (1975) *Frieden und Völkerrecht*, Stuttgart: Klett.

Pocock, John G.A. (1975) *The Machiavellian Moment*, Princeton: Princeton University Press.

—— (1991) 'Deconstructing Europe', *London Review of Books* (19 December).

Pohl, Frederic and Cyril Kornbluth (1953, 1981) *The Space Merchants*, Harmondsworth: Penguin.

Pollard, Sidney (1982) *The Integration of the European Economy*, London: Allen & Unwin.

Pratt, Edwin A. (1915) *The Rise of Rail Power in War and Conquest*, London: P.S. King.

Price, Roger (1990) 'France, the search for stability', in Bruce Waller (ed.) *Themes in Modern European History*, London: Unwin Hyman.

The Radical Programme (1885, 1971), London: Harvester Press.

Raffarin, Jean-Pierre (1988) *92 Europe: Nous Sommes Tous des Régionaux*, Paris: Projets Editions.

Read, Donald (1964) *The English Provinces*, c. *1760–1860: A Study in Influence*, London: Arnold.

Reulecke, Jürgen (1993) 'Das Bergische Land als Pionierregion der deutschen

Industrialisierung', in Schulze (ed.) *Structural Change in Early-Industrialised Regions*, Essen: Klartext Verlag.

Reulecke, Jürgen and Gerhard Huck (1981) 'Urban history research in Germany: its development and present condition', *Urban History Yearbook*, 39–45.

Ribhegge, Wilhelm (1991) *Europa – Nation – Region*, Darmstadt: Wissen-schaftliche Buchgesellschaft.

Robbins, Michael (1970) *The Railway Age*, Harmondsworth: Penguin.

Robson, W.A. (1935) 'The outlook', in Harold Laski, Ivor Jennings and W.A. Robson (eds) *100 Years of Municipal Progress*, London: Allen & Unwin.

—— (1971) 'The missing dimension of government', *Political Quarterly*, 42, 3 (July), 233–9.

Rokkan, Stein (1980) 'Territories, centres and peripheries', in Jean Gottman, *Centre and Periphery*, London: Sage, 164–99.

Romero, José-Luiz Curbelo (1987) 'Economic restructuring and regional development in the underdeveloped regions', *Journal of Regional Policy*, 4, 37–56.

Rommelspacher, Thomas (1993) 'Wasser und Abwasser in der Region Ruhrgebiet', in Schulze.

Rougemont, Denis de (1977, 1983) *The Future is Within Us*, Oxford: Pergamon Press.

Rousseau, Mark O. and Raphael Zariski (1987) *Regionalism and Regional Devolution in Comparative Perspective*, New York: Praeger.

Rubenstein, W. (1981) *Men of Property*, London: Croom Helm.

Salveson, Paul (1990) *The People's Monuments*, Manchester: Workers Edu-cational Association.

Sampson, Anthony (1968) *The New Europeans*, London: Hodder & Stoughton.

Sartre, Jean-Paul (1971) 'The Burgos trials', *Planet*, 8 (October-November), 3–21.

Schama, Simon (1987) *The Embarrassment of Riches: An Interpretation of Dutch Culture in the Golden Age*, New York: Knopf.

Schlenker, L.H. (1987) 'Local industrial strategies: a key to French economic planning in the eighties?', *Comparative Politics*, 19, 3 (April), 267–72.

Schöneweg, Egon (1993) 'Ausrichtung und Leistungsfähigkeit der Regional-politik der Europäischen Gemeinschaften', in U. Bullmann (ed.) *Die Regionen im EG-Integrationsprozess*, Giessen: Giessen University Press.

Schröder, Helmut (1991) 'Geschichte der Berufsausbildung: Ein Überblick', Karlsruhe University, unpublished paper.

Schulze, Hagen (1985) 'Die Stern-Hardenbergschen Reformen und ihre Bedeutung für die deutsche Geschichte' in *Pressen*, Stuttgart: Klett-Cotta.

Schulze, Rainer (ed.) (1993) *Structural Change in Early-Industrialised Regions: A European Comparison*, Essen: Klartext Verlag.

Schumacher, E.F. (1973) *Small is Beautiful*, London: Abacus.

Serant, Paul (1970) 'The Rise of French Regionalism', *Planet*, 2, 16–18.

Shand, James D. (1984) 'The Reichsautobahn: Symbol for the Third Reich', *Journal of Contemporary History*, 19, 2 (April), 191–6.

Sherrington, Emlyn (1980) 'Welsh nationalism, the French Revolution, and the influence of the French right, 1880–1930', in David Smith (ed.) *A People and a Proletariat*, London: Pluto Press, 127–47.

Sillars, Jim (1985) *Scotland: The Case for Optimism*, Edinburgh: Mainstream.

Simon, Sir E.D. (1939) *The Smaller Democracies of Europe*, London: Gollancz.

Smith, Adam (1776, 1952) *The Wealth of Nations*, New York: Encyclopaedia Britannica.

Smith, Graham (ed.) (1991) *The Nationalities Question in the Soviet Union*, London: Longman.

Smith, Paul (1991) 'The Alsatians and the Alsace-Lorraine question in European politics, c. 1900–1925', in *CS*, 5, 59–83.

Stares, Paul B. (ed.) (1992) *The New Germany and the New Europe*, Washington: Brookings Institution.

Steinberg, Jonathan (1974) *Why Switzerland?*, London: Faber.

Steinberg, S.H. (1966) *The Thirty Years War*, London: Edward Arnold.

Stengers, Jean (1990) 'Belgian national sentiment', in René Bryssinck (ed.) *Modern Belgium*, Brussels: Modern Belgium Association, 190–6.

Stern, Fritz (1987) *Dreams and Delusions*, London: Weidenfeld & Nicolson.

Stewart, A.T.Q. (1977, 1989) *The Narrow Ground*, London: Faber.

Streit, Clarence (1939) *Union Now*, London: Cape.

Strikwerda, Carl (1989) 'The Paradoxes of Urbanisation: Belgian Socialism and Society in the *Belle Epoque*', *Urban History Yearbook*, 82–96.

Stumann, F. J. (1990) 'The regions of Europe: from regionalisation to regionalism', *Magazine of the European Regions*, No. 1, Strasbourg: Assembly of the European Regions.

Sturm, Roland (1988) 'Das Vereinigte Königreich von Großbritannien und Irland: Nationale Identitäten, regionale Besonderheiten, politische Konflikte', in Hans-Georg Wehling (ed.) *Regionen und Regionalismus in Westeuropa*, Stuttgart: Landeszentrale für Politische Bildung Baden-Württemberg/Kohlhammer, 22–45.

—— (1990) 'Industriepolitik auf regionaler Ebene: Optionen einer konservativen Redefinition regionalisierter Förderstrategien im deutsch-britischen Vergleich', in W. Krumbein and U. Jürgens (eds) *Industriepolitik im Vergleich*, Berlin: Edition Sigma.

Tamse, Coenraad (1985) 'Belgium and the Netherlands: small countries in the nineteenth century', in *Rapports*, 2, Stuttgart: Comité International des Sciences Historiques, 417–20.

Taylor, A.J.P. (1941, 1976) *The Habsburg Monarchy*, Harmondsworth: Penguin.

Thomas, Dafydd Elis (1991) 'The Constitution of Wales', in B. Crick, *National Identities*, Oxford: *Political Quarterly*/Blackwell, 57–67.

Tocqueville, Alexis de (1835, 1954) *Democracy in America*, New York: Random House.

—— (1958) *Journeys to England and Ireland*, ed. J.P. Mayer, London: Faber.

Topf, Richard, Peter Mohler and Anthony Heath (1989) 'Pride in one's country: Britain and West Germany', *British Social Attitudes*, London: Gower, 123–40.

Towndrow, F.E. (1941) *Replanning Britain* (Oxford Conference Spring), London: Faber.

Wallas, Graham (1914) *Human Nature in Politics*, London: Constable.

—— (1920) *The Great Society*, London: Constable.

Waller, Philip (1981) *Democracy and Sectarianism*, Liverpool: Liverpool University Press.

Ward, A.W., G.W. Prothero and Stanley Leathes (eds) (1910) *The Cambridge Modern History, 7: The Latest Age*, Cambridge: Cambridge University Press.

Watson, Michael (ed.) (1990) *Contemporary Minority Nationalism*, London: Routledge.

Webb, Sidney (1910) 'Social movements', in A.W. Ward, G.W. Prothero and Stanley Leathes (eds) *The Cambridge Modern History*, 7: *The Latest Age*, Cambridge: Cambridge University Press, 730–66.

Weber, Eugen (1979) *Peasants into Frenchmen: The Transformation of Rural France*, London: Chatto and Windus.

—— (1991) *My France*, London: Belknap.

Wehling, H.V. (ed.) *The German's Southwest*, Stuttgart: Kohlhammer.

Weiss, Linda (1989) 'Regional economic policy in Italy', in C. Crouch and D. Marquand *the New Centralism*, Oxford: Blackwell, 109–24.

Wells, H.G. (1908) *New Worlds for Old*, London: Constable.

Wiener, Martin (1981) *English Culture and the Decline of the Industrial Spirit*, Cambridge: Cambridge University Press.

Wilkinson, James (1989) 'The uses of popular culture by local elites: the case of Alsace, 1890–1914', *History of European Ideas*, 11, 605–18.

Williams, Raymond (1985) *The Country and the City*, London: Chatto & Windus.

Williamson, Arthur (1979) *Scottish National Consciousness in the Age of James VI*, Edinburgh: John Donald.

Wood, Ian S. (1989) 'Hope deferred: Labour in Scotland in the 1920s', in Ian Donnachie, Christopher Harvie and Ian S. Wood (eds) *Forward! Labour Politics in Scotland, 1888–1988*, Edinburgh: Polygon, 38–40.

Index